BLESSED to SERVE

LESSONS LEARNED AND STORIES SHARED FROM TORCH-BEARERS OF MODERN YOGA

DUNCAN WONG SIANNA SHERMAN JASON CRANDELL
RUSTY WELLS STEPHANIE SNYDER DARREN MAIN
KATHRYN BUDIG GEOFFREY RONIGER JASON NEMER

Karen Lo

INVERSIONS INC.

Turning the world around, one yoga teacher at a time.

Inversions Inc. produces high-quality educational materials for yoga teachers, and the larger yoga community. Find out more at www.InversionsInc.com.

Published and distributed by Inversions Inc: www.InversionsInc.com

Copyright © 2012 Karen Lo
(All photograph copyrights remain with the photographers)

ISBN: 978-007212575-7

Printed in the United States of America

❧ DEDICATION

> A teacher affects eternity;
> he can never tell where his influence stops.
>
> ~*Henry Brooks Adams*

To the many inspirational teachers I've had in my life so far, and to those that have yet to come. Like a rain drop's ripples in a pond, there's no telling what your wisdom will touch.

❧ CONTENTS

"Unconditioned by time, (The Source) is the teacher of even the most ancient teachers."

- The Yoga Sutras of Patanjali

ॐ Introduction

This is an age where we have instructional DVD's, Yogaglo.com and international yoga conferences. Facebook pages and websites are an expected part of the yoga teacher's professional arsenal. How does modernity interface with yoga? What happens to the yoga *tradition*? The "commercialization of yoga" has inspired many recent heated debates within the community, but it is not such a new topic. There have been numerous incidents throughout its long history that triggered questions of propriety, ownership, and authenticity. These are some of the questions that this book explores.

As seekers, our path is never entirely clear. Often only the next step is revealed to us. We follow with as much faith, trust and surrender as we can manage. Even if we are blessed to have clarity as we forge ahead, the path is never without challenge. When we remind ourselves that this very challenge is actually the gift, we can shift in perspective and soften our stride. This allows us to live in the flow of the river, float in the magic of our practice, and find the most precious and truest gift, ourselves.

Meditation teacher Jack Kornfield tells the story of Tibetan teacher Chöyam Trungpa Rinpoche when he was late to a talk in Berkeley. He offered anyone who wanted a refund to get one. He then said, "In fact, if you haven't started the spiritual path, best not to begin! It's difficult, it's terrible, and you will have to face all kinds of things that you won't like." He continued, quite seriously, "If you don't even start, you'll probably be better off. Best not to begin. But if you do start, best to finish!" Ready or not, we are all already on the path. We can move forward kicking and screaming, or with courage and tenacity. Luckily, we don't have to go it alone. The teachers in this book lend their wisdom to us.

Inspiration for this book came from my quest to understand what it means to be at once a seeker, student and teacher. While I was managing a successful yoga studio in San Francisco, I realized that that there were many wonderful, well–trained, loving and passionate yoga teachers hungry for advice and knowledge on how to proceed on their path. They needed guides, or at least some sense of shared experience. There are many books and workshops on asana, and on spirituality, but there is little available about what it's like to be a modern–day yoga *teacher*. What are the challenges and pitfalls? What are the joys and gifts? How do you navigate your own growth as a yogi while guiding others along their path? Sometimes, the teachers at my studio would ask me tactical questions: "What should I do besides have a website?" or "I've put postcards in café's, what else should I do?" But it seemed to me that they needed more experienced teachers to share their wisdom on these topics.

This project began with the intention of helping yoga *teachers*, but I quickly realized that teachers are yoga *students* first. The most brilliant gems revealed by the interview process shared in the following pages were not advice specific to teaching, but simply words of wisdom about being a yogi in the modern day. Kathryn Budig, one of the youngest faces on the yoga scene said, "It's that mixture of living with magic in your life, but also having some firm feet on the ground." And Rusty Wells inspired the title of this book when he talked about the responsibility of yoga teachers who are "blessed to serve."

I feel strongly that having yoga in my life is a privilege, and I'm blessed every day to practice both on and off my mat. Yoga is an ancient tradition with spiraling lineages and a family tree that branches off in more directions than we can count. Part of our responsibility as practitioners is to not only acknowledge lineage, but also familiarize ourselves with yoga's history and cultural context. There's great benefit to simply doing your salutations every morning—this speaks to the power of yoga. But it has even more impact if you know that it's traditionally a salute to the sun God, Surya, and that this tradition has been passed down for generations as a way to begin your day. As we take yoga into the future, it behooves us to delve more deeply into our practice so that we can be true to both our lineages and ourselves.

➤ State of Yoga address

Yoga scholar Georg Feuerstein notes in *Yoga Philosophy and History* that study of yoga is more than 6,500 years old, if you include the early accounts of Vedic and non-Vedic history. He classifies the most recent epoch of yoga as "Postclassical" (after 200A.D.). That's still a whopping 1800+ years of yoga tradition. Today, if you ask a new practitioner what "yoga" is, they will probably describe something that is exclusively the modern postural practice; the physical part of the tradition. According to yoga historian Mark Singleton in *Yoga Body*, what most of us think of as "yoga" is actually fairly new, and derived directly or indirectly from Krishnamacharya's lineage of hatha yoga.[1] These practices have had mixed influences, including Scandinavian bodybuilding and British military exercises, many of which were incorporated during the turn of the twentieth century.

Yoga is always changing, and it will continue to evolve as we evolve. It has growth spurts, just like all other cultural/spiritual/philosophical movements, and I believe that we are in one of those fertile periods now. It is an exciting time to be practicing yoga. It's more accessible than ever, there are more choices and options than ever before, and you don't need to renounce your "regular" life to do it. What does this mean for the yoga tradition as a whole?

I was fortunate to talk with Beryl Bender Birch in the course of researching this book. Beryl was one of the first women to teach Ashtanga yoga on the East Coast during the early 80's. She is the bestselling author of *Power Yoga* (1995), a groundbreaking book that unintentionally led to a falling out with her teacher, Pattabhi Jois. *Power Yoga* was publicly criticized by Jois in a published letter to *Yoga Journal* for being inauthentic. Beryl's intention was always for Ashtanga yoga to be accessible to a new population of students. In my candid interview with her, she spoke of the pain she went through when the book was released and received so negatively by Jois and some of his students. "I was working with athletes and they were seeing yoga as wimpy, stretchy, and not serious. And here I was, doing Ashtanga, and holy cow, it's a ferocious practice. It is

---

[1] Sri Tirumalai Krishnamacharya was a yoga teacher and healer who opened the Mysore yogashala. His students include B.K.S. Iyengar, K. Pattabhi Jois, Indra Devi, A.G. Mohan, and his son, T.K.V. Desikachar. Many historians attribute the modern postural practice we know as yoga largely to his innovations, teaching and the subsequent teachings of his students.

powerful; this is a serious discipline. And I wanted people to know that one, it was a workout; two, I knew that Western minds could relate to the words 'Power Yoga'; and three, I felt that it would be really beneficial to athletes." While the term "Power Yoga" probably wouldn't set off any alarms for today's practitioners, it was certainly controversial in its time, not so long ago.

When I asked Beryl to give advice on how to be devoted to our lineage while being true to our own inner compass, she said, "That's kind of the quintessential question of life. How much do you surrender? How much do you let go? And how much do you hang on? When is it appropriate to hang on and be firm and stand your ground? When it is appropriate to back off, let go, surrender, and soften? It's a balance between hard and soft...you can draw your line wherever you want." She went on to say that in many ways, none of us can really teach yoga. "Yoga is what happens to you when you're able to quiet your mind and nobody can put it into words. It's spiritual, beyond description, infinite, eternal, connecting with The One. And when you experience it, it will blow your mind." In that spirit, this book provides reflections on hard lessons learned, stories of inspiration, and maybe even some practical advice on what it's like to be, as Darren Main says, an "urban mystic."

Let us find guidance and gain perspective from those who've walked the path before us. As Stephanie Snyder said, "No one can really ever *tell* you anything." You have to experience it for yourself.

❧ Torch-bearers

Deciding who to interview was difficult because there is such a plethora of wise and knowledgeable voices in the yoga world. As I refined the topic of this book, I realized that the questions I wanted to ask pertained more to teachers who have had the experience of interacting with modernity in an active way. Perhaps it was through their bestselling DVDs, global travel, or Facebook campaigns, though they may elicit mixed feelings. And so I set out to identify who those teachers might be.

Not by any strict parameters, I've chosen what I call the "second generation" of American yoga teachers to be the subject of this book. The "first generation" includes trailblazers like Ramanand Patel, Maty Ezraty & Chuck Miller, Rodney Yee, Amrit Desai, Tim Miller, Norman Allen, Beryl Bender Birch, and Judith Lasater. They started teaching at a time when there was very little yoga in the US. They had a unique struggle: to bring something "foreign" to Americans, often straight from gurus in India, to the US. There were no such things as yoga studios, much less what now seems like one on every corner in cities like San Francisco, New York, and Los Angeles. They probably couldn't have imagined a multi-story, multi-studio center with over 100 classes per week like the Integral Yoga Institute of New York.

Now, what we see is a generation of yoga teachers who are "homegrown" – having predominantly studied in the US. These torchbearers often bring yoga to new populations and even to other countries around the world. What these teachers have in common is that they are faced with challenges like large (or extremely large) classes, online connection with students, yoga marketing, corporate yoga programs... the business of yoga on a level that we've never seen before. "Second generation" is used broadly here since even within this category of teachers, there's a multitude of experience and approaches.

The advice and opinions they offer are not always in agreement. The benefit of having such a diversity of voices is that we realize that there isn't necessarily one right way, just a right way for us. But there were also many striking similarities in what they said. One thing that I found moving was their view that being a yoga teacher is a *calling*. Also, you not only should, but *must* teach from your authentic self. This is actually the key to truly compelling classes, and meaningful connection with students. Each of these teachers, in their own way, speaks *so* honestly and passionately! It was clear to me exactly why they do what they do. Together with Shiva Rae, Seane Corn, MC Yogi, Janet Stone and many other dedicated yoga teachers, they bear the torch of modern yoga.

❧ A responsibility to pass it forward

I feel like I've been given a gift, and it's actually my responsibility to pass it on. As I set up interviews, I knew I would be sharing them in the form of this book... but after each interview, it was different—it was a visceral feeling—I realized that I was being freely given such remarkable wisdom by these dedicated teachers. And so, I'm passing on their words with deep gratitude and a sincere hope that you will be as inspired by their words as I have been. They are alive in me—may they be alive in you.

In the spirit of giving back, a portion of the proceeds of this book will be donated to Give Back Yoga Foundation, *a non-profit organization that supports yoga teachers bringing yoga to underserved communities.*

❧ Chapter 1

Stephanie Snyder

Stephanie is the creator of the Yoga Journal DVD, Yoga for Strength and Toning, *and is known for her inspirational teaching style. Students appreciate Stephanie's unique ability to infuse her flowing Vinyasa classes with yoga philosophy, concise technical alignment, and heart- felt humor. Her commitment to breath, movement, happiness, and prayer make Stephanie one of the country's most sought after teachers.*

Stephanie teaches workshops, classes, retreats and teacher trainings globally as well as locally in her hometown of San Francisco, California.

You can find Stephanie presenting at the Yoga Journal Conferences, teaching online vinyasa and prenatal classes, and in a town near you. Stephanie humbly and enthusiastically sits on the Board of Directors for Headstand, a non-profit organization dedicated to integrating Yoga into the curriculum at schools that serve at-risk youth around the country. She also regularly supports and fund raises for multiple other non-profit organizations.

She has been interviewed and profiled by Yoga Journal magazine, YogiTimes magazine, Fox News, and InStyle Magazine among many others. She has also been a contributing writer for and featured on the cover of Yoga Journal Magazine.

<hr />

If you've ever seen a photo of Stephanie Snyder on the cover of Yoga Journal or any other magazine that she's graced the cover of, you know that she's beautiful. And she was even more glowing in her pregnant state when we sat down together to talk on one of those rare sunny San Francisco days. But what is so striking to me about Stephanie is actually her slightly brassy and wonderfully straightforward manner. I felt immediately like we were confidants and that she was being very "real" with me. Hanging out at a local café with Stephanie over brownies and tea felt both like an event and like we'd done it a hundred times before. Her honesty only added to her knack for making the people around her really comfortable, which is perhaps why her weekly classes are often filled with more than 200 people.

❧ It's like a blackout!

Karen: How did you decide to be a yoga teacher?

Stephanie: I was really into yoga and was working in an office. I'd gone through some major life changes and sort of just one day thought: "I've gone through so many hard times and gotten to this really great place in my life. I work so hard for clarity on what my life needs to be, and it's just too short and precious for me to spend ten hours a day doing something I don't love." I had no intention of teaching yoga. That wasn't even in my realm of possibility. But I was doing tons of yoga, I loved yoga and I didn't know what I wanted to do, but the sales job wasn't it. So I thought I'd do a teacher training because it was 30 days of yoga and I'd be steeped in my practice. I thought that being so connected to the practice would help me figure out what I wanted to do with my life. And I honestly don't know what happened after that, it's like a blackout! [*we're laughing*] And here I am. That's it. One thing led to the next, it just unfolded.

I do remember the first year I taught yoga, I made thirteen grand. And I lived on that. I would buy a burrito in the Mission [in San Francisco] and I'd eat the first half for lunch and the second half for dinner. That's it. I lived like that for a year. I lived in this tiny apartment in the Haight [-Ashbury District]. My roommate had rent control since he'd been living there for 15 years. I was already paying *low* rent and I told him that I was probably going to have to move because I couldn't afford it and he actually lowered the rent for me, so I could keep teaching yoga.

19

Nowadays, you look at a studio like Yoga Tree, they're doing three or four teacher trainings a year with something like forty people each. I mean, do the math. That's just one studio, and they're not the only ones. There's just masses of teachers coming out. And students are like, "It seems like there's a lot of competition, it looks really hard." And I just think, you know what, if it's meant to be, none of that matters. So if it calls to you, you go for it. And if it doesn't work out, you try something else. It's sort of out of your hands. The competition should be irrelevant. What other people are doing is none of your business. That's a good mantra. I don't know how it worked out, but I just ended up teaching. But I do have to say that when I started teaching, it was a much different market.

K: How was it different?

S: There was only one teacher training in the Bay Area. One. It was only once a year. I mean, nobody was teaching yoga. You were committing to a life of poverty if you were teaching yoga. There was no business behind it like there is now. Getting a job was much easier though. It was like, no big deal, unlike nowadays. Now you have to have a resume! If I had to have a resume, it never would've happened. [*we laugh*] So it's very different.

K: Do you remember your first class?

S: Well, I don't remember my first "real" class that people paid for. But I remember that I showed up to teach my first class that you do as part of the teacher training program, and I was so nervous. It was a public class, but they knew that I was a trainee, so there wasn't *that* much pressure. You have a mentor who's evaluating you and I got there, stood there for a minute, and turned to my mentor and was like, "I can't do it. I'm really sorry, but I just can't do it." I really couldn't do it. She said, "Okay" and had to teach the class. It took me like two weeks to get my shit together. And then I showed up and taught that class. I just got through it. It was very nerve wracking for me; *so* nerve wracking in the beginning. But I still enjoyed it, and I stuck with it. And I kind of feel like as long as people keep giving me the opportunity, I'll keep saying, "Yes." And one thing just led to the next. I feel super grateful [*she knocks on the table*] that lots of things have fallen into my lap.

ꙮ Wearing different hats

K: Where do you think yoga is in its growth?

S: I've heard that it's a *billion* dollar business these days. I don't know, it's huge and growing, which is great. I love that it's growing because it serves everyone so well. We'll see what happens. My first relationship to the practice is always as a student. As far as I'm concerned, that's my main priority. As for the business end of it, I'm just really grateful that this is what I get to do for work. I'm glad that the business is growing, I'm glad that it's a business that I get to be part of. I don't consider myself a big business person, I just figure it out as I go.

K: What about the traveling aspect of it?

S: I love to travel. I love meeting all these different yogis, seeing different studios, and just connecting with community all over the place. But ever since I had my son, it's a lot harder to be away. So I'm really paring down. This year, I traveled once a month, I will probably do less next year because I'm having my second baby. The baby will be new and it'll just be a lot more technically challenging. Luckily at this point, I have some good community around the country. I don't have to set that up. I just show up and they take good care of me. But it's always a balance.

K: Do you travel with your son?

S: Usually, I do not. I usually fly in and fly back. Boom boom boom. I feel like if he's with me, I'm sort of not doing a great job being a mom and not doing a great job of being a yoga teacher. Know what I mean? So it's better for him and for the students if I'm doing one thing and not the other. It depends  on the scenario. He could've come to Wanderlust, he can come if it's going to be fun. But I don't want to drag him around and he has to wait around for me to teach. He'd rather be home with his friends or at school where everything is normal. That works best for us.

One thing Dharma [Mittra] used to say—and he travels a lot more now, he didn't travel much for a long long time—he said that the sad thing is that nobody has a teacher anymore; because the teacher gets big and then they leave. And then they travel all year around. And it's true. The teachers don't stay local once they get to a certain point. They're just sort of on the road. Maybe they teach here and there, maybe one or two classes or something. Maybe eventually, there'll be enough of us that we can all just teach locally. And people could just come to us. That'd be nice. But it's a global world that we live in.

❧ The Sacred Contract

K: Being a global world, and with traveling to teach, do you think it changes the student/teacher relationship from "back in the day"?

S: I think that the student/teacher relationship remains intact because it's a sacred contract that we're all in. I mean, past lives and all of that. One of the big differences now is that there's a [direct] exchange of money. Traditionally, first of all, it was all orally passed on, which it still should be for the most part, but the community would also take care of the teacher. There was an ashram and the teacher would be fed and housed and whatnot. But that's not how it works now. There's an exchange of money and that sort of changes everything. So that changes the student/teacher relationship to a degree. But it doesn't change the essence of what the relationship should be. I think that if everybody respects the practice first, then the rest sort of falls into place and stays where it should be.

K: For the teachers like yourself who have bestselling DVD's, I'm sure there are students you've never met who write on your Facebook wall about how much they love you…

S: It's amazing, it really is. Here's the thing, I have a love/hate relationship with technology because I think that for the most part, it isolates us. However, there are ways that it's connecting us too. What's cool is when I go to workshops in

DC or some other city in the country and someone comes up to me and says, "I've been practicing with your DVD for like two years and now I finally just took your class." And we connect through that. That's wild! That's really crazy, and it's really cool. And it *is* a way to connect. Facebook is a way to connect. I don't troll around and look at people's pictures because there are parts of Facebook that probably aren't healthy for us. But yeah, that's one way to connect.

And Yogaglo[.com]—the website that has all the classes online—they're really committed to making it a community. Students can chat and comment on there and the teacher can chime in. They're committed to using technology to connect instead of isolate. It gives greater access, and access is good, as long as we don't rely on that alone. I don't think we will because there's nothing like being in a class. Technology is good for convenience but it'll never replace the real thing, it's just a supplement. If you believe in reincarnation and karma or even in some Buddhist philosophy, if someone is connected to me through my DVD, we've been connected in other lives somehow anyway. You know what I mean? In some ways, it's not *that* spectacular.

❧ No one can really ever tell you anything

K: If there was one thing you wish someone would've told you when you first started, what would that be?

S: I don't know that anyone could've told me anything that would've made sense then, that I'd like to know now. This doesn't really answer your question, but I think that I was a little bit unprepared for the business side of yoga. It's a business like any other business. There are the same sort...um...we're humans and when money's involved, it becomes more complicated. You kind of feel like, "It's yoga," but it's also business and there's always a bottom line. I've encountered people who handle that with more grace and people who handle it with less grace.

K: Like who?

S: Anybody involved. Yoga teachers, studio owners, media. Anyone who's making anything from it. It's a business. So I think I had to wrap my brain around that. I was in sales, and I felt like I left that for a reason. But I just realized that well...business is business. But I don't think anyone could've given me any advice that would've made sense then.

K: Because you figured it out as it happened?

S: Right! No one can ever really tell you anything, right? In the moment, about your future, because you don't get it, or you're not able to receive it.

❧ Let the practice serve you

K: What do you think is the best thing about being a yoga teacher?

S: How close I get to stay to the practice. I get my whole life to be "yoga." I get to have everything I read and do support my practice. And it supports my personal practice and my professional choice.

K: Do you ever feel like not practicing?

S: Of course. Everyone feels like not practicing. I struggled with that in the beginning because I was an Ashtanga practitioner...you know, I try to say this to my students...several times a week I will start class with them in downdog, I set them up and then I say, "Just move your body for a few breaths and do whatever feels right." And I tell them that *that*'s the practice at home. You get on your mat, put on some music that you love and then just move your body and trust what comes through.

What keeps us from practicing is that we think it has to be five surya namaskar A's, then five B's, then I have to do my sitting poses or whatever your lineage is. And I think I got to a point where now, even if I don't feel like practicing, I want to practice because it'll make me feel better. My practice is vinyasa, but I do a lot of somatic movement, restorative, and now, prenatal.

Through the years, you kind of grow up a little bit in the practice and realize that the practice serves you and you don't have to serve the practice. If you feel like you have to serve the practice, it's too much work! But if you really get that the practice is to serve you, then it's like a warm blanket, it's very nurturing, it's supporting you. There are times that I don't feel like practicing, but I still want to, if that makes any sense. And then I do what feels right. Sometimes it's a short practice, sometimes it's a long practice. Sometimes it's easy, sometimes it's really hard, and that all feels great. So I just let it be what it needs to be, and that helps.

❧ Be yourself

K: What's the best advice you've ever gotten?

S: Geez, I should've reviewed your questions.[*we laugh*] Okay—this is easy. The Bhagavad Gita, Chapter 3, "Be Yourself." That's the best advice I've ever gotten and I could give anybody. Everything unfolds from there. That's it.

❧ So go, do it

K: What would you say to a student who's thinking about becoming a teacher?

S: Just go for it, yeah. Why not? If you love yoga *that* much, then just do it and see what happens. I mean, that's the path. Our job is to do our practice, figure out how we can become happy and free from suffering. Or at least lessen our suffering through our practice. That practice reveals something to us. And we're not really happy until we reveal that to someone else. That's our job—it's to learn and then teach. That's the natural progression of the practice. Which is partly why there's so many teachers on the market now and so many people going into teacher trainings. It makes perfect sense. So go, do it. And then it'll manifest in whatever way that it does.

❧ It's not me they're coming for

K: How do you handle the huge classes? Because you've got some big classes.

S: I know. I'm totally shocked every time I walk in the room and see *that* many people have shown up. Every time, I'm like, "Wow, this is amazing." I handle it the same way that I handle a very small class. Same energy, same connecting. I had 300 people this weekend at Wanderlust. You just find more shakti.

I do remember getting really excited and a little overwhelmed when I was a new teacher, and I had three or four people in most of my classes back then. And we were paid like three dollars per person, so I taught something like twenty classes so I could make my little tiny rent. I never want to take credit for the big class thing. It's the practice, it's just the practice. It's a partnership between me and the students. It's the yoga they're coming for, it's not me. And you just get used to it like anything else. I'm just grateful that there are so many people doing yoga and they're willing to cram in like that, for the sake of the practice.

We're so lucky here in San Francisco. We're such a strong yoga community. And not just strong in terms of commitment and numbers, but physically, we're a very young, strong, group of yogis in this city.

K: What are some of the differences that you see in traveling from city to city?

S: I look at it not so much as city to city but more studio to studio. Every studio has its own personality. That's true even within San Francisco. You just sort of get to know them, and get to know it as a whole. It's great, I love it. Every studio is a little different that I go to. It's nice to travel and get to see that. You get to see all the different bodies and these different people. Some people aren't necessarily practicing every day, but they're still really committed to the practice and really interested in it and want to learn more. They're grateful for the practice and for their one studio. The one studio that's within a twenty-mile radius. It's really neat to see that.

❧ Start comparing, suffer instantly

K: What do you think about all the different kinds of yoga popping up?

S: I think over time we might remember that there's no ownership. We need to balance that truth with the fact that there is a way that you develop or present the information in your own voice, and it's okay to identify that.

K: We have had very strong lineages like Iyengar, Ashtanga, but every teacher teaches their own way…

S: We do. But all of us have a teacher and that teacher has a teacher and I think what makes me sad is that's been lost. Crediting your teachers has been lost a little bit. I think it kind of dilutes a really beautiful part of the practice, which is the passing on. Dharma Mittra's my teacher and I've had many teachers in the past. Tias Little is someone I've studied with recently and I credit him. I've learned so much from him even though I haven't studied a ton with him. I have definitely gained a lot of knowledge that I then pass on to my students.

I don't want to say that's mine. And I'm sure he wouldn't say it's his either. I hope that doesn't get completely lost, the honoring of teachers.

K: Any last words of advice?

S: The main thing to communicate for newer teachers…is to trust. There's no need to get grabby or work too hard at promoting. I really think that your teaching stands on its own. And you always attract people that you're meant to attract. You can't sit around and do nothing. But at the same time, I think some people have become so consumed with the promotion stuff that it's too much. And they're working too hard. Stop working too hard, cut it out! *(laughs)*

And you can't compare. You start comparing and you suffer instantly. Whether you're comparing and thinking you're better or comparing and thinking you're worse. It'll lead you directly to suffer. The sutras say, no matter what someone else is doing, to condemn them is even worse. Just let it be, you're not in charge of anybody else. No one's in charge of how yoga should be. You do what works for you and that's that. That's the best thing.

For more about Stephanie,
visit www.StephanieSnyder.com

❧ CHAPTER 2

JASON CRANDELL

Jason Crandell was recently named "one of the next generation of teachers shaping yoga's future" by Yoga Journal for his skillful, unique approach to vinyasa yoga. Jason's steady pace, creative sequencing, and attention to detail encourage students to move slowly, deeply, and mindfully into their bodies. Take a class from Jason and you will leave feeling grounded, clear, and content—and more informed of the nuances and habits of your body and mind. Jason credits his primary teacher, Rodney Yee, teachers in the Iyengar Yoga tradition such as Ramanand Patel, and ongoing studies in

Eastern and Western philosophy for inspiring him to bring greater alignment and mindfulness to vinyasa yoga.

In the past 10 years, Jason's "knack for explaining subtle body movements in a way that anyone can understand," (Yoga Journal) has opened many doors. Most recently, Jason created two Yoga Journal DVDs, Yoga for Wellbeing *and* Your Complete Home Practice Companion: Yoga for Morning, Noon, and Night. *He is a contributing editor for Yoga Journal and has written over 13 articles for the magazine and website—many of which have been translated internationally (including in Japan, China, Italy and Brazil). Jason teaches extensively at conferences in the United States and abroad and is part of numerous teacher-training faculties. He has recently partnered with Yoga Journal to continue creating high-quality, home-practice DVDs.*

Jason's integrative and accessible teachings support students of every background and lineage, helping them to find greater depth, awareness, and wellbeing in their practice—and in their lives.

—⁓—

Talking to Jason makes you want to stand up straighter and go immediately to work on your asana and breathing. That's not to say that he's a taskmaster. On the contrary, he has a wonderfully dry sense of humor, a quick wit, and talks you into complicated poses through sequencing that's never harsh or sudden. The quality and tone of his voice and his particular style of cueing has inspired many a yogi to follow him with dedication. It's not hard to see why this is.

❧ Yes, I'll take them

Karen: How did you come to decide to be a yoga teacher?

Jason: You know, I always jokingly answer this and say that I didn't have any other prospects. [*we laugh*] I have an undergraduate philosophy degree and I always expected to be in education and academics. So, for as long as I remember, I thought that I would be a teacher of some sort. I just wasn't clear on what the subject matter would be. I didn't know if the subject matter was sociology, or history, or philosophy or what. Whatever it was, I figured that I'd be involved in some sort of intellectual engagement and some sort of education, and that was that.

And it wasn't until one of my teachers in the mid-90's said that he was going to let go of his Introduction to Ashtanga classes and asked if I would be interested in taking them, that I even considered teaching yoga. I'd never gone through a teacher training program. But I said, "Yeah, I'll take them." And as soon as I started teaching them—I'm really bad on dates but I think it was '98 or so—I realized that I was just in over my head, that I just didn't have the skills to be an educator. I knew what *my* practice felt like, and I knew how to deal with people pretty well. But I didn't understand the basic mechanisms of teaching and connecting with groups of people. And then I started studying more with Rodney Yee and joined his eighteen-month teacher training program, along with other faculty, and that was it. It just grew and grew. That program really supported and fomented everything to come.

K: And has it turned out differently than you'd originally thought?

J: It has continued to grow and evolve in interesting and significant ways. But honestly, I don't know what I expected, I really don't. I feel very fortunate. I feel like I'm lucky enough to have a group of students who resonate with me and I resonate with them. And that has grown and deepened over the years. But I can't say that I anticipated this and I also can't say that I'm easily surprised by very much. Again, rarely would I say that I have no expectations. For better or worse, I have a lot of expectations of a lot of things. This was just something that I didn't. This was just something that I didn't see coming and at the same time, it seems to be a pretty good fit.

❧ I kept a second job

K: What were the first few years of teaching like?

J: Poor. You know, hard! Really, really hard. You don't make much money, you have ridiculously low self-esteem. For me, I just spent a lot of time not knowing whether or not I was teaching clearly and whether or not students were receiving things that were valuable to them in their lives. So there was a lot of doubt. I mean, a lot of doubt as to whether I was being clear and whether or not there was some sort of connection. And a lot of, and I mean, a *lot* of hard work. There was a lot of subbing at really terrible times and really small classes. I always kept a second job, definitely.

K: Were there moments that although hard, were worth it?

J: It was always worth it. Now that doesn't mean that I didn't have significant doubt, I often have significant doubt. Honestly, it's only been the last couple of years when I have let go some of that systemic doubt. Wondering whether or not I'm in the right place, doing the right thing. But it was always immensely rewarding. It forced me to do my practice and look inside. So it was always incredibly valuable—even with lots of doubt.

❧ Let's get physical

K: Where do you think yoga is in its growth?

J: You now, I think it's flattened, to be quite honest. From what I've seen, Asia and Europe have become more popular epicenters of yoga. But I see that the rate of new people doing yoga has decreased. But I think the amount of people who *are* practicing, has become more consistent. So it's a more, for lack of a better term, a more mature marketplace. It's not quite as "boom" as it was in terms of the total number of new people arriving, but I feel like it has become a consistent, regular, sustainable thing in countless peoples' lives. I feel like it has stabilized.

K: What about in regards to style? Do you think it's going to be different in the future?

J: I think that people will continue to use yoga as a practice to navigate the vicissitudes and the challenges and the questions of their lives. And so, I think it will continue to stay relevant to what people need. There are countless varieties of yoga because there are a lot of different people with different

Photo: David Martinez

personality types who are using the practice to meet their specific needs. So I don't think yoga will change per se, but I don't know that yoga *has* changed. How people employ it will continue to shift as it continues to meet the needs of people; as people continue to shift and change.

One of the needs a lot of us have is to be very physical. The West, especially, has a very physically sedentary life. And sometimes certain yogas get a bad rap for being "just physical." But by God, we need it! We need something that's really physical. People are being physical for like, an hour a day, maximum. So of course we've embraced the more overtly physical practice. People spend all day in office environments; they need to do something that is robust and physical. So I would assume that as cultures continue to shift, people will continue to use this practice in slightly different ways to meet their needs and decrease suffering.

From teacher referral to the facebook age

K: What's your relationship to technology like?

J: Definitely mixed. I'm doing my best to embrace it, but I have to say that I have some fear and anxiety regarding how important technology is becoming as a marketing medium. You know, I've been fortunate enough to go through a lot of traditional channels, like teacher recommendations. That's sort of how teachers used to get more exposure. It was direct teacher referral, lineage. That's being bypassed, big time. You don't really need direct lineage approval or direct teacher recommendations or approval to have really enormous exposure on Facebook, YouTube or other mechanisms. The anti-authoritarian in me loves that. I love that people can market themselves and have greater access to exposure. But the part of me that really loves the editorial process is a bit scared, to be quite honest.

K: In a similar note, do having people in class who've originally gotten to "know" you through your Yoga Journal podcasts change things for you in the classroom?

J: Well…first, a bit in contrast to what I just said, I do have to admit that technology has been very favorable to me. And those podcasts, they were one of the major ways that have helped people find me. I pitched those podcasts to Yoga Journal years and years ago! I just realized that they were going to be a very efficient tool to teach people for free, people I wouldn't be able to teach in other situations. I can teach people from all over the world through those podcasts. I feel very fortunate that I've been able to leverage the technology that exists, even though I have a mixed relationship to it.

A lot of people do come to class who have "interacted" with me before. And that definitely sets a precedent, and sets up a certain amount of expectation. It also sets up a little bit of separation. It's like there's a feeling that they know me, even though they don't know me. They'll recognize my face, recognize my voice, and my cueing. There's a little bit of a surreal quality when they then get to come to class and meet me in person. They've interacted with me in a different medium and now they're interacting with me in a real time medium. And it's just a little bit strange. But I don't think that it significantly changes what they expect in class nor is it harder for me to live up to expectations. I don't really think it necessarily gives me the benefit of the doubt or an upper edge with regards to authority. Interacting with anyone in multiple mediums is strange for the mind.

K: Does this change the teacher/student relationship for you?

J: I'm fortunate enough to have essentially three groups of students. I have the students that I see almost every week, in person. I have the students who I see once a year at a workshop or a conference or whatever the locale is. And then I have students that I interact with—actually quite a bit—online. From Yogaglo[.com] and from the Yoga Journal podcasts. I don't know that we have a relationship; we have an internet relationship which… I don't even know what that means! All I know is, there are people whose names I am familiar with who comment on my classes online and email me and ask me questions online. And I do my best to respond and interact and genuinely engage with the online community. And I like it! It's not nearly as intimate as me being able to see them, and know them, and adjust them in downdog. And at the same time, I can think of 10–15 names of people off the top of my head that I interact with regularly online and I have never seen or talked to them in person. And that's actually pretty satisfying as a teacher. You know, my fundamental goal as a teacher is to be an educator and I'm willing to use whatever medium is available to me to help facilitate whatever degree of education I can help facilitate. And it seems to be valuable.

❧ Teach from your heels, not from your toes

K: What's the best piece of advice you've ever gotten?

J: It was probably in the first conversation that I ever had with Rodney [Yee]. He'd already gotten a pretty good sense of who I was and what my nervous system was like, and how my mind operated. I'd been his student for a period, I was in his teacher training program, and he's incredibly perceptive. We were having lunch and he looked at me and said, "You're going to have to learn how to teach from your heels and not from your toes." And he meant by that—or as least how I've interpreted it—is that I need to step back and observe and see what's happening in the room and be responsive. Rather than pushing pushing pushing an agenda, and trying to expedite a specific reaction or transformation in the group. He could see that I have a certain degree of intensity and the capacity to over-teach. And he saw that for me to be good, I needed to just let the class come to me, rather than forcing it. He probably gave me that advice 12 years ago, and I would say that specific mental note, of teaching from my heels, comes up in my mind at least once a week. And it has, once a week, for 12 years. And it's something that I continue to try to do because it's something that's actually difficult for me.

K: What do you think is the hardest lesson you've learned in your career?

J: Do I just have to pick one?! [*we laugh*]

There's a couple and they're related. I think the first thing is that in regards to success—however one measures success—I used to think that once I had a certain amount of students and once I had a certain amount of exposure... I used to think that once a teacher had a certain amount of respect and popularity, that it just stayed that way. And it doesn't. It's like, people will tend to think "Oh, if I just get to teach at a conference," or "If I just do this workshop at this popular studio" or "If I just assist this well-known teacher then students will like me and come to class regularly and I'll be able to hang my hat on that." And the truth is, maintaining the respect that you cultivate requires much more work than getting it in the first place.

Photo: David Martinez

The second thing is that you're going to be a match for some students, and you're not going to be a match for other students. No matter who you are and what you do and how you teach and how much you care, some students just aren't going to resonate with who are you and what you're doing. There's no way that you can make everyone happy. It's such a familiar refrain but as yoga teachers, we sincerely want to help, we sincerely care, and we can't help *everyone*. It's a pretty glaringly obvious lesson that we teachers learn time and time again.

❧ It's actually Dharma

K: What would you say to a student who's thinking about becoming a teacher?

J: Always remember that you are an educator first, and that you get the opportunity to continue to practice the art of teaching. As newer teachers, we usually start to put pressure on ourselves for what poses we can do, how strong we are, what our body looks like, what knowledge we have cultivated, and how much we know. Some of those things are valuable, but what we have to actually do is practice teaching. To actually consider what goes into teaching, what goes into communication, what goes into sequencing and what goes into relating well to students and seeing them clearly and practicing the skill of observation. You actually need to practice the skill of communicating and teaching.

And don't quit your day job too soon. It's too much stress and pressure to expect to have a lot of students and tie all of your income needs too early to teaching yoga. It's a hard vocation with regards to the actual logistics of making a living. It's hard and it takes a long time.

K: Is there one thing that you wish someone would've told you when you'd first started?

J: Be very patient and figure out what is the most important thing you want to teach as a yoga teacher. And just dedicate yourself to teaching that thing. As opposed to being too caught up too soon in popularity, numbers, this studio, that studio. You know, *the* thing that will sustain a yoga teacher for a long period of time is dharma. It is actually dharma. It isn't popularity, it's dharma—feeling like there is a deep essential thing or set of things that you are working to communicate. And then you'll be satisfied when you skillfully communicate that thing. It's about dharma.

For more about Jason,
visit www.JasonYoga.com

❧ CHAPTER 3

Jennifer Graham Photography

SIANNA SHERMAN

Sianna is an internationally recognized Anusara Yoga teacher who delights in sharing these teachings as an offering to the Divine Mother. Her parents and sister have been her life-long inspirations of embodied love. In 1990, Sianna began traveling the world to study the art of yoga. Her travels spanned the continents as she delved into the richness of the great traditions of yoga

In 1993, while traveling in India, she followed a series of dreams that guided her to Ganeshpuri where she met Gurumayi Chidvalasananda. In this blessed ashram, she began her first conscious studies of Tantra, which ignited her entire being like a living flame. Just a few weeks earlier, she had celebrated her birthday by sitting on a boulder in the currents of the Ganges River contemplating her life, listening to the water and hearing the promise within to follow the path of her heart. This inner listening guided her to a most exquisite meeting with her primary mentor John Friend in 1995 and two years later, John founded Anusara Yoga. She apprenticed with John for many years and continues to be near him as much as possible.

In 2008 she was chosen by Yoga Journal as one of 21 talented young teachers who are shaping the future of yoga. Known for her artful fusion of heart, alignment, therapeutics and creative sequencing, Sianna facilitates a sacred space for each person to feel held in a wider embrace of compassion and love. She shares her insights in the way of stories, personal experiences, poetry and yoga philosophy rooted in Tantra. Sianna has a special devotion to collaboration, community and collectively conscious gatherings that help elevate the vibration of humanity. As a regular contributor to Yoga Journal, YogaGlo online yoga, Origin Magazine and other multimedia expressions, she wishes to serve the students with accessible information that helps them in the true transformation of their lives.

Sianna humbly bows to all her teachers on this path of Grace, especially to Gurumayi Chidvilasananda, John Friend, Douglas Brooks, Paul Muller-Ortega, Bill Mahony, Hareesh Wallis, Christopher Tompkins, all her priestess teachers and sisters, and her Open to Grace family.

—◦◦◦—

Sianna's unbridled energy is palpable, even before you speak to her. You only have to be near her in order for you to feel the electricity in the air. She frequently uses the word "shakti" and it's no wonder as she's fully charged with expansive energy that's simply infectious. And once you're sitting down talking to her, she draws you into her circle effortlessly and with ease. She's warm and funny, abounds with heartfelt advice and since she fully believes in you, it's easier to believe in yourself.

❧ Dr. Sherman?

Karen: How did you decide to become a yoga teacher?

Sianna: I was actually en route to medical school and I decided to defer for a year to go travel the world before I committed the next ten years, or more, of my life to my career. I was going to combine a PhD in Nutrition what a MD, so that it could become my own program of integrative medicine, which didn't really exist at the time. The year before, I'd been in New York City and was at the dance clubs, which is something that I loved, and I got locked out of my friend's apartment. It was the middle of the night and really cold, when I found an all night book store that was open. I walked in hoping to find something that would capture my attention. This book started to literally fall off the shelf, right on top of my head, and I caught it! It was called *The Power of Your Subconscious Mind*. [*we laugh*]

I sat down and read that book cover to cover in that one night. I thought: "Why didn't anyone tell me about this?" I felt like those teenage years were hard years for me, I felt like I was sabotaging myself. Whether it was body image, or the pressure to do really well in school, or to get into medical school. There was so much pressure in every direction and I felt like I was losing myself, that I didn't know who I was. So when I started to first explore yoga and meditation and the power of the subconscious mind, I was looking for an internal alignment. I started to ask the questions: What does happiness really mean to me? What does the world expect from me? What do I really want for myself? So when I took that year off, it was quite a powerful year.

I ended up studying meditation and yoga, moving to a macrobiotics community, and I began exploring various alternative modalities. I put on a back-pack and traveled through Europe. At some point, I was working at a health food store—and this is how the yoga/asana part comes in—and I kept seeing these people walking out of a house across the street with yoga mats, but I didn't even know what they were at the time. [*laughing*] So one day they came in and I noticed that they seemed very happy; there was a buzz about them. So I asked them, "What's that?" And they said, "It's a yoga mat." I asked them, "Where's the class?" And they told me that it was on the top floor of the house across the street. The next week was my birthday and I gave myself the present of eight yoga classes, and that's how it began. Obviously, I never made it back to medical school, although I kept thinking that I would. I even went to naturopathic medical school for a while, then I studied Ayurveda and nutrition, then I became a massage therapist and just kept learning as many modalities as I could. But the yoga kept deepening and ripening and it just became everything, a full lifestyle.

K: So the teaching just came naturally?

S: I didn't even think about it. I always taught in some capacity. I apprenticed with many yoga teachers, took lots of different styles and different teacher trainings, and then people just started asking me, "Will you teach me? Will you teach me? Will you teach me?" I remember I was at a women's herbal conference and they saw me practicing and asked if I would be their yoga teacher for the conference. I said yes, and it just kept happening.

The teachers that I was apprenticing with began asking me to sub their classes. It grew very organically. It just kept offering itself to me. I knew that my life was dedicated to yoga, I knew that from the beginning. I think I knew that as early as 19 or 20 years old. I just didn't know in what capacity. Then in my early 20's I met Gurumayi Chidvilasananda and shortly after that, I met John Friend, and shortly after that, I started apprenticing with him and going on the road with him. It just kept igniting; it was like a wild fire. It was really beautiful.

The first years of teaching were like this; "organic" is a good word. Then in 1995, a manager of a yoga studio in Eugene, Oregon, really needed a teacher. They found out about me, even though I lived quite far away, and there were suddenly numerous classes available that they really wanted me to help orchestrate on a big level. So I just made the leap and for that year, I really gave myself to the yoga studio. That was the first year with real structure around teaching. The few years before that were much more loose and about following a pulsation, a rhythm. It was like the Shakti was orchestrating it all and I just followed Her lead.

❧ Yoga in the yellow pages

K: Where do you think yoga is in its growth?

47

S: Yoga is booming. Honestly, I would've never thought it would become so mainstream and available. I mean, when I started like 23 years ago, I had to search for it. I had to go out and search, as in the Yellow Pages. [*we laugh*] Even in a big city like Chicago, I had to really go searching for where to take a yoga class. It's kind of incredible to see what's happened. It's booming! It's entirely ignited everywhere. I grew up in a small Midwest town in Kentucky and now yoga is everywhere there too. All my friends and cousins know about it. When I first started, they were all like: "*What* are you doing?!" And now it's primetime.

It's grown in the way of business, that's for sure. But what's really happening is that yoga is meeting people on the planet right now in a way that they need to be met, and in a place that they need to be welcomed into. Yoga's also providing a method to be in touch with yourself, in a way that can also open up to community. It's always been a very personal, private, and rich practice and it still is. But now this is a highly creative collaboration as a community, with festivals igniting with music and yoga. It's opening up into extraordinary celebration with people everywhere. And I think that this is what our planet needs right now, because people are feeling disconnected. There's so much pressure and global intensity and disharmony. People, in their spirit and in their hearts, long for companionship and they long to have peace, and to live their life in the way of love and something greater; a remembrance that we all belong to each other really.

K: Do you see this across lineages?

S: I can only speak from my perspective, but there's all these rich lineages of yoga and traditions that are masterful unto themselves, *and* they're opening up a wide embrace to each other. I just taught at Wanderulust last week and I co-taught several of my classes with AcroYogis Jenny and Jason, with Shakti Sunfire hula-hooping, with tantrik scholar Harresh Wallis. All these things are coming together. I was at a festival prior to this where I taught with Saul David Raye and Janet Stone–they're both of different lineages; we all love each other and we love to teach together. We want to represent our lineages, so to speak, but then activate them and embrace each other, and create a rich vibrant matrix. There are these different traditions but it's all just one tradition too.

❧ The Real Teacher

K: As far as we know, in India, the yoga tradition was usually passed from guru to disciple, guru to disciple, etc. But now, we see teachers like John Friend, who might have 500 or even 1000 people in class. Do you see the student/teacher relationship being different now?

S: It's both. It's the same in that there is always the discipleship to "shakti." "Shakti" means power and it means a transmission of energy in that everything is alive. And shakti becomes embodied as the teacher. Everyone is in discipleship to the Maha Shakti.[2] So in that sense, there's this one-on-one relationship. Some students find just

Photo by Nicholas Callaway, Turquoise wrap by Hanuman

---

[2] Maha Shakti: The Universal Mother.

one person as a teacher and have this really close, personal relationship. Back then, you found your teacher and you sat one-to-one and learned together. But because yoga is now so large in scale, it's the same relationship but it has to be transmitted through the field of a lot of people. It can be one to 500 sometimes. You would really think that it would dilute the transmission, but it can actually also build the transmission, when the teacher is truly plugged in and connected to their source as they're teaching. Even when you look out and see this infinite sea of people, when the teacher just plugs in and remembers the bigger source energy and the Universal, that transmission comes through.

It's the Maha Shakti who's really the teacher. She comes through the vessel of the teacher and reaches and touches everyone. And everyone can have a very personal relationship with the teachings in this way. Because the real teacher is Maha Shakti.

❧ Stand tall in the light

K: What's the best advice you've ever gotten?

S: Inner body bright. That's from my teacher, John Friend. It's actually from the lineage of his teacher through the Siddha yoga tradition, and all the way back to Bhagawan Nityananda. This is a great question. If you've ever seen photos of Bhagawan Nityananda, he is literally a beaming, extraordinary vessel of light and pure pure shakti and total love. John used to meditate on his photos a lot, and would look at him and thought that Nityananda had the best alignment he had ever seen, without ever having taken a hatha yoga class in his life.

So as John contemplated and meditated on his photos, he started to realize that it should be called "inner body bright." And this is what we say in Anusara is the first principle. "Opening to grace, inner body bright. Outer body soft unto this light."

What "inner body bright" means and why I say it's the best advice is because no matter how intense my life can become,  John will say "Sianna, inner body bright." And it's his way of saying: "It doesn't matter what's happening on the outside. No matter how fierce and intense and up against ourselves we feel, if we tap into that place—the place that yoga guides and invites each one of us to—we'll find that our essence is bright and that our inner freedom is fully present." Often, it's our outer freedom that's compromised by our own mind. We say: "Oh I'm not free" or "I'm a victim, I'm not empowered." Or, "This happened to me…" and we start to close down. And that's easy to do, but if we go inside and wait a minute, there's this inner freedom that's never compromised; there's this inner light that's always true. So you say to yourself, "Inner body bright, let me melt the outer body, melt all the crazy stuff that's happening into the fire of my heart, into that inner light and then I'm going to stand tall in this light and keep going, no matter what." I think it's the best advice I've ever gotten.

❧ Authenticity and vulnerability

K: Is there something that you struggled with in your career?

51

S: I really wasn't super fond of speaking in front of people. [*we laugh*] I wasn't at all. I can remember being in high school and college and having to do those presentations, and I just didn't like it. I didn't want to have to stand up in front of people and have to speak. So I went to my dad and he said, "Look, it's hard for you because you don't really believe in what you're talking about. They're asking you to talk about something that you don't really believe in. I promise you that the day will come when you care about something so deeply and it'll really mean something to you, and these fears will just naturally fall away and you'll be able to do it."

And that happened through yoga. I can remember those first classes, thinking: "I still don't want to stand up here in front and talk to people while they all have their eyes on me." But then, this beautiful thing happened: I plugged into myself and I just spoke the truth of what was real for me, inviting people to this place within themselves. And my dad was right: all of a sudden it became effortless.

There were many years of struggle up until those moments, and that was a tough lesson, but one of the most extraordinary lessons because it taught me about authenticity. I struggled so much before, for different reasons. For one, I wasn't really speaking about things that lit me up, or that I cared very deeply about. Two, maybe I thought that I had to speak in a certain way or say what I thought the teacher wanted to hear or what was going to get me the best grade. And here you are in yoga, and it's all about authenticity. You're speaking with your authentic presence and your authentic voice and inviting that into the students' hearts. And in that place, the fears just start to fall away. So it was a lesson about authenticity and how truly powerful it is. It was also a lesson in vulnerability; to let ourselves be vulnerable and real with what is. And that's how the human heart connects, vulnerability and authenticity allow for true intimacy and for transmission, and for the heart to awaken in each other's company.

❧ Your heart's longing

K: What would you say to a student who's thinking about becoming a teacher?

S: I would say that if it's your heart's longing, if it's really your calling and your heart's longing, then go for it. It's one of the greatest services that can be provided at this time and if you really have that calling then you will be so thrilled to take the seat of the teacher. Remember that as you take the seat of the teacher, you are first and foremost taking the seat of the student, because every student will be your teacher. Every single teacher becomes even a greater student of the shakti, the Maha Shakti. We're all in discipleship to—however you want to speak about it—to the universal, to the one love, to the Goddess. But we are in the highest studentship as teachers. Once you choose to become a teacher, your own studentship gets catapulted exponentially to the highest level. So be ready, and go for it, and be the best student you can be so you can really serve fully.

❧ Follow your heart

K: If you could go back in time and tell the old Sianna something, what would that be?

S: Geez, I've had so many great beings along the way that guided me. As cliché as it is, it's simply "Follow your heart." When I started all of this, I was going the academic route. A lot of people thought that it was the better idea, that it made more sense. "Why don't you become a doctor first and then become a yoga teacher?" [*laughs*]

Most people couldn't really understand why I would make this choice. And it was several years later that I was meditating on a boulder in the middle of the Ganges River, early morning up near Rishikesh, in India. I was sitting on a rock and the river was flowing all around me and I was praying and meditating and I remember distinctly writing in my journal, "From this day forward, I commit myself to the path of my heart. No matter what." And it was my commitment to myself. I was still in the struggle of feeling like maybe I was making the wrong choice, that maybe I should just be going to medical school. But there was too much resistance.

So I think the advice is: You really do know. If you feel resistance, you have to sit with this resistance and feel it for what it is. Ask if the resistance is in your mind. Is it real? Is it something you should be paying attention to? Or is it being placed upon you by other people's thoughts and expectations? So as clichéd as it is, follow your heart. Listen deeply. *You really do know.*

Find the most resonant teachers for you, the best guides, because they do open up the pathway and lead you; It's because they've walked the path that they can lead you. But ultimately, you just listen within and listen so deep, that you know the truth of yourself. And follow it, be bold, be courageous, really go for it! When you do, it's the highest, and everything else will follow in its wake.

Learn more about Sianna
at www.OpenToGrace.com

ꙮ Chapter 4

Rusty Wells

Rusty practices, teaches, and lives Bhakti yoga - the yoga of love and devotion. Balabhadra, a devotee of His Divine Grace A.C. Bhaktivedanta Swami Prabhupada, first introduced Rusty to this practice in 1990. This compassionate spiritual master followed Lord Krishna's teachings found at the heart of the Bhagavad-Gita: Bhaktya mam abhijanati (18:11), which means "I can only be known by devotional service." In addition to Bhakti, Balabhadra also taught him the importance of selfless service, Karma yoga; and chanting in a group or softly to oneself, called Japa and Kirtana.

Rusty began his practice of Hatha yoga in 1996 through the teachings of Masters Swami Sivananda and Swami Vishnu Devananda, who emphasized the synthesis of asanas (postures), pranayama (breath exercises), relaxation, and proper diet to develop the physical body and awaken the energies. They also taught selfless service to remove egoism; mantra chanting and worship to release emotion into devotion and selfless love; study of the scriptures to transcend the intellect, and meditation to go deeply within and arrive at the true nature of our being-Self, God, the Truth. Rusty has been teaching in the San Francisco Bay Area since 1998 and enjoys fusing together the many wonderful influences he's had from teachers such as Pandit Rajmani Tigunait, Georg Feuerstein, Sri Dharma Mittra, Baron Baptiste, David Life, Sharon Gannon, and everyone who has ever demonstrated patience and exquisite kindness - including every single parent who somehow 'keeps it all together'. Their eclectic methods inspires his teaching and continues to deepen the experiences of his own personal practice. Ashtanga, Bikram and Jivamukti are important systems within the diverse practice of yoga. Inspired by these methods, he incorporates certain elements from each into his own practice and instruction. While Rusty's classes tend to be vigorous and physically challenging, their actual power stems from each student's internal experience. He encourages all to recognize that a generous, compassionate nature gives us the wonderful opportunity to transcend our limits and let go of what no longer serves us. With that realization, we can release our egos and prepare our hearts for the opportunity to be of service through unconditional love and devotion.

—∾—

Watching Rusty hug and talk to his students after his class was such a sweet thing to witness. There was so much respect and love for one another; there was more in the air than your typical post-yoga class bliss. Rusty has a reputation for an intensely devoted following. I was at a dinner party not long before this interview where someone expressed the sentiment that Rusty's personality is very magnetic. But the second that we started talking, it became apparent that he's very much human, and incredibly wise and unusually sweet. Sure, it's accurate to say that Rusty is very charismatic, but one of the most striking things about him is his ability to really embrace you with his energy. Also true is his down-to-earth-ness and a kind of "wise neighbor" sensibility that made his words easy to absorb.

❦ The inner compass

Karen: How did you come to decide to be a yoga teacher?

Rusty: Once I began to practice yoga, I couldn't shut up about it. I found that it had taken over my life — the whole practice — and I *could not shut up.* My passion really ignited when I would share with my friends and anyone on my path. When someone in my life had a problem or something they were particularly interested in, I would share what little bit I knew from my experience with yoga. I just couldn't help it. Then, someone from a small studio recognized something in me, and asked if I would fill in to teach one day. They knew that I'd taken a short training program. At first I said, "I'm not ready yet." This teacher looked at me and said: "You're ready." And so I taught that one class, and then took on a regular class, and then I took more training, and then I took on more classes... until I had to finally get rid of my day job. It took a little while, but not too long. Just exactly the right amount of time, actually.

K: It sounds like you fell into it. Did you have expectations going into it? Or were you just pulled by your passion?

R: The inner compass, it led me straightaway. It wasn't like I was looking for extra income, or wanting to fill my time. I was already working fulltime, and I loved my job. I was really busy. But I've always found that yoga, when we love it, will make its own space and time in our lives. Always. And it creates its own fit into our lives, really sweetly. Whether on the mat or off the mat. Whether it's practicing or teaching — it accommodates. But I actually came into the practice itself kicking and screaming. I never wanted to do yoga. In fact, I was a rebel, not a joiner. But I had two friends nag me so much that one day I gave in, went to my first class, and then I went back every day after that. *[we laugh]*

K: Do you remember what class it was?

R: I do. It was a Sivananda class. And I fell madly in love with this fairly traditional form of hatha yoga. It let me get away from a competitive edge that I'd always felt when working out and doing sports. In those activities, I'd felt like I needed to compete with others and my own expectations. And I battled with that just about a nanosecond on the mat. Then it went away, and I was left luxuriating in that feeling of letting my body move freely and carefully. It was quite wonderful.

K: Many teachers I've talked to make it sound like there was a call.

R: When something knocks on your door and you miss it, it's hard to go back later and get it. But if you're really listening and you're in tune and you're asked, you're drawn into it as a service, basically. As a teacher trainer, I've seen people come into training programs specifically hoping to get big, create a huge following, and have a lucrative income. That's their main objective. I have learned to weed out these folks right off the bat. Sometimes, these things are a byproduct of being a good teacher, but there's no guarantee. Who knows? Who knows if people will even come to your class? First, you have to love your practice. You must want to share it and do something good with it. A teacher should be fed by the opportunity to serve... at least, that's been my own experience. I don't encourage any brand new teacher to drop their day job and expect to teach yoga right off the bat. You have to meld into it, gradually and carefully, and always make sure you're taking of *yourself*. Only then can you take care of others.

❧ Keep it organic

K: What were the first years of teaching like?

R: When I first started, I would write out my sequence. But that rarely worked. For me, it never worked, actually. I have colleagues who write out everything; they know exactly what they're going to do, and this works great for them. But for me, I'd have these grandiose ideas, and then I just wouldn't feel it when I was teaching. It didn't feel like the vibe of the room, or what the students wanted to do. So I became more organic and spontaneous in my sequencing. And that's where freestyle Bhakti Flow vinyasa yoga came from. It was perfect, and I've always loved it very much.

One caution I give to a lot of new teachers is to be careful to not try to over-promote yourself too early, because you need time to get in there and mess up. You need to teach to preferably a small audience of friends and family that you can use as your guinea pigs. To really learn, to develop, and to make sure you have everything you need in your tool kit. It's a vast amount of knowledge that you need. You need to know about anatomy and physiology and special situations for special students. You need to know a bit about yoga philosophy and history and maybe even a little Sanskrit. It's a lot of information for a new teacher, and it's very hard to come in and prove everything to a large group.

I developed a large student base quickly, and that kind of freaked me out. At some level, I felt like I wasn't ready. I wasn't finished studying yet. So I made that my task. Every day I studied, every day I practiced yoga, every day I tried learn something about this practice, or I unlearned it. Or I tried to rethink something. Nothing trippy or heavy, but enough to keep it fresh and interesting and always remind me that first and foremost, I'm a student. For new teachers, make sure you're taking the time with this and paying it the homage it deserves.

❧ A long-lasting fad

K: Where do you think yoga is its growth?

R: You know, it's funny, because I thought maybe ten years ago that the fad was going to fade. It hasn't. It's been incorporated into daily life for so many people and there are always new students coming. There are so many interested in the practice. I just haven't seen it wane at all. In fact, I've seen it constantly grow. Whether it's in our city — which is already robust with yoga — or Indonesia, The Netherlands, or Belgium or many other places, there are constant newcomers to it everywhere.

I love working with teachers who are in the more outlying communities. They're the pioneers, because people in those areas don't really know much about yoga, but they're starting to get interested. These new teachers, they're just so brave! It melts my heart. They're bringing yoga to a small community that really doesn't know if it's interested in it yet. And I watch how, over the course of even just a couple of years, it blossoms. We take it for granted here in San Francisco. There's a yoga studio on every corner. And then you look at a town that's never had yoga, and some brave being says "I want to start teaching yoga," and then they open up their living room or take over a little shop, and they just let it happen. I see it all over the world. I've been teaching in Greece for eight summers now. I remember when there wasn't a great interest in yoga there. I met some students who were just starting to get interested in trying to find a teacher training for a weekend so they could teach in a gym. That's all anybody wanted. They had humble ambitions. And now there's a huge community in Greece that practices and treats their practice with a lot of respect, and now they have longer training programs. They've really done justice to the practice. I think it's growing, like crazy, still. This is one long-lasting fad.

❧ I've just got the good playlist

K: Do you think that the student/teacher relationship has changed over the years?

R: Personally, *I've* changed since I started teaching. So I don't know if *it's* changed, but I've changed. When you're a new teacher, it's easy to let people fawn all over you. Quickly, I learned that that's not healthy for anybody. I'm not here to be served; I'm just someone who's here to turn on the music and to direct an experience that's for the wellbeing of everybody who's here. As a new teacher, it's very easy to get brought into this ego feed, but after a little bit, you start to detect that it's not healthy. I try to remind students and myself of the great teachings — especially from *The Bhagavad Gita,* where Krishna is constantly reminding us that we're equal. Every being is equal. There's the same amount of God in every being. Nobody has any more than anyone else. So I don't personally believe in the guru complex.

I think of myself merely as an instructor, because I don't know that I actually have that much to teach. I can share my life experiences and what is precious to me, mostly because of the loss that I've had in my life. And I can share what's of great value that maybe can help you appreciate it as I do, what we have right here and now. And that is probably the purest lesson of this life. To really count our blessings while they're right smack dab in front of us. You know, this is the precious part of the practice, to be so present that we see what we have and adore it. And try not to cling too tightly to it. We embrace. So if someone else has a different notion of what they need from me, then I try and explain that that's not why I'm here.

I'm here to celebrate this practice together as a community. I just happen to be the one with the good playlist and some creative sequencing ideas that I sometimes remember to teach on both sides, sometimes not.

❧ Know your stuff, and apologize later

K: What's the best piece of advice you've ever gotten?

R: *[laughs]* Really? The best piece of advice has got to be: "It's better to ask for forgiveness than for permission." Absolutely. This comes in handy frequently. Because I keep finding myself wanting to ask, "Oh, would you mind…?" And then I think to myself, "No, just do it. Just do it instead, and if need be, apologize later." I don't mean this to be careless. Not at all. But I think this helps me stay very brave. I hold this true even with my practice on the mat. Patanjali tells us: sthira sukham asanam. Keep a strong foundation but maintain comfort all the while. I think this is great. As an instructor, I never *tell* people to do anything, I'll encourage it, and ask that folks give it a try. And if it doesn't connect, I'll say "Oh, sorry about that." And this seems to work fine. People tend to be very kind and generous when they know they are well-supported. I remind folks that if something ever feels like it's too much, they are the one choosing to do it.

K: If there's one thing you wish someone would've told you when you first started teaching, what would that be?

R: Make sure you know your stuff. I mean, really. Make sure you know it. Because you think you know it, and like I said, all of sudden you're subjected to not just a growing student community, but within that there's a community of teachers who come in and want to see what you're all about. And then you hear the harshest things, and they're totally legitimate. Because you're still budding, still growing, still learning. Maybe you don't know everything that you need to know. So I'm going to say that it would've been nice if somebody had stopped me early on and said, "Time out, time out. Lets have you check in about a few things. Makes sure you've got this together." But I feel like I've done well. I haven't killed anybody! I've taught a few thousands people since I started, and nobody's dead yet.

❧ Take time for yourself

K: What's the hardest lesson that you've learned in your career?

R: I think it's important to be able to take time off from teaching. You should be able to give yourself a little time to rejuvenate, to restore, and even just to study and practice with somebody else for a little bit. If your career is teaching, you're an independent contractor, usually, and taking time off isn't easy. But when you feel your energy being drained, or when you feel like you need a little recharge, I think it's important to take that space and time to feed and feel oneself. It's really tough, too, because you want to stay consistent and be there for people. But it's probably important to be able… you know what? It *is* important to be able to give yourself permission to take time off.

K: Maybe because when you teach a ton, you start to lose connection with the practice.

R: And that's when you slip into autopilot, when you just go right in and "Dah, dah, dah...... *chaturanga*." And you're not even really there. I'm absolutely present when I teach. I can honestly say, no matter what weighs on me, by the time I walk in, I just see who's in front of me and I set my own stuff aside. There's no talent in that; it just happens organically. I can set whatever it is that's weighing on me over here *[gestures to the side]* and let myself be immersed in the present time energy.

I'm so fortunate, I'm so blessed to be surrounded by good, happy, generous people. I feel very lucky. So it's easy to walk right into that and be a part of it. And then, if by chance, I have something weighing on me, I keep it to the side for a bit, and when I come back to it later, it's usually smaller, maybe tiny even. It's a win-win situation. If you catch yourself going into autopilot when you're teaching, *stop*. You may be doing more harm than good. To yourself, to your practice, and to the students you're blessed to serve. Just pause and go to a mentor. Rather than a guru, I recommend mentors. I don't mind being a mentor for newer teachers and students. Someone who's basically just been down the street a little longer.

❧ But I can't touch my toes!

K: What would you say to a student who's thinking about becoming a teacher?

R: I had someone once ask me, "I want to be a teacher, I really want to share this..." and I knew this person, this student. I could clearly see his passion, and he said, "...but I still can't do *uttanasana*. I still can't do forward fold. How can I teach yoga?"

And that was powerful for me. I said, "I don't care if you can execute the pose. I really don't, because you know what it's like to try." I would rather have a teacher who knows what it's like to be on the journey than one who is already at the presumed destination. I once studied for a while with a teacher who was an acrobat, dancer, and a phenomenal stretchy contortionist type of person. There were three of us in class; we were in standing forward fold (uttanasana) and she said, "And now just float up into handstand." And we all looked at her like, "What?" I mean, still, to this day, I need to be in down dog to kick up into handstand carefully. She looked back at us with no empathy, like, "Just do it." And I looked back at her and thought, "You're not the teacher for me. You have no idea who I am, and you have no idea what we're doing here." I would rather study with the person who can't touch his toes, but who can share with me what it feels like to try. You know? That, to me, is much more sacred. It's much more real; it's much more connected to my own experience.

K: What do you think are the necessary ingredients to being a good teacher?

R: Well, you need some charisma! I don't even know if you can go get that anywhere. I think that it may just be self-confidence, to a degree, but maybe it's also belief in what you are doing, belief in the basic message. I love the asana practice, but that's not why I'm in this. I'm in this to raise up myself, raise up my family, raise up my community a little bit. To remind everybody that this is a sweet, noble, kind, and very short life. It will be gone. And I don't want to look back with regret. There's so much sadness and isolation, even with people walking around smiling all the time. And I just think, "Ah…" Sometimes your yoga mat can awaken you to that place of being so present that you actually see the blessing of your life.

I'm not religious. I'm in an ever-evolving state of appreciating what I have in my life. And I'm connected to a divine power that doesn't have a form that I know of. I see it in moments of my life and in flickers of just being so present with another being or even with myself, or with my dog, or with the sunset. It just comes to me and makes me feel like I'm really at home. And that makes everything quite okay. The practice of a teacher who is just starting up requires confidence. You should believe in it. And remember, you can't be a teacher without students. If you really do believe in the practice, then stand tall, be brave, and share it unapologetically. Offer it with all of your heart.

For more about Rusty,
visit www.RustyWells.com

❧ CHAPTER 5

DARREN MAIN

Darren Main is a yoga and meditation *instructor and author whose life experiences have inspired him to help others to traverse the difficult road of being seekers in modern day. His sense of humor and sensitive touch allow students to be free to open their hearts and bodies. Darren finds that sharing the experiences that have led him to a life of spirituality and embodiment is powerful medicine for students who simply need to connect.*

Darren's first yoga class came shortly after his eighteenth birthday when he reached a low point in his life. He had been using sex and drugs as a way to cope. Realizing that he was burying his pain in things that offered only a temporary reprieve, he began to search for a way to live in peace with himself and the world. Ellie Brown, his first yoga teacher, changed his life forever. He was soon led to seated meditation and then to A Course in Miracles (ACIM). Through these modalities and the help of his friends Michael and Jasper, Darren found his path.

Darren's formal study included massage therapy at the Bancroft School of Massage and yoga teacher training at the Kripalu Center for Yoga and Health. In 2002, he began leading yoga teacher trainings including the 200-hr certification program at Yoga Tree in San Francisco. Teaching others to teach yoga—then watching them share yoga with the world in their own unique way—inspires him to continue delving into his own practice.

As an author, Darren's books include Yoga and the Path of the Urban Mystic, Spiritual Journeys along the Yellow Brick Road, Inner Tranquility, Hearts and Minds: Talking to Christians about Homosexuality and his latest book, The Yogi Entrepreneur: A Guide to Earning a Mindful Living through Yoga. He facilitates workshops and gives talks on yoga and modern spirituality throughout the United States and abroad. He is the host of the syndicated podcast Inquire Within. He currently resides in San Francisco. He classes include a donation-based practice at Grace Cathedral.

⬥⬥⬥

Darren Main is very real. He's hilarious, warm and inviting. As we sat on his living room floor together and talked, I more than once found myself almost rolling on the ground laughing. At the same time, his spiritual nature and his genuine desire to help is also right there on the surface of everything that he says. As an author of several books, he has a way with words and his analogies strike right to the heart of things. Darren is not afraid to speak his mind and his convictions are fair and decisive.

～ The yoga dog whistle

Karen: Even as the yoga community grows, there's still a sense of competition among yoga teachers. What do you think about that?

Darren: I always say, you as a yoga teacher have a unique voice. It's like a dog whistle that only certain students can hear. You know there's that saying in India, "When the student is ready, the teacher appears." But there are also a lot of students out there just waiting for the teacher to find their own voice. And most often young teachers may say, "Oh! Rusty Wells or Janet Stone, they're super popular, I'm gonna do what they do." But then you're competing with them, when maybe your calling is working in a senior citizens home [*laughs*] or something else. Your students might be people who would never go to Rusty's class because…he loves to chant, and some people love it and some people don't. So if you don't want to chant, don't. You don't need to.

K: So authenticity is the way to go?

D: Yes! Otherwise, you're also setting yourself up for failure. If you put yourself up there as this Guru, who can do anything, who never makes mistakes, you will, because you're human. And when you fall, people will hate you. You don't have to show everybody your dirty underwear, but don't deny that you have it. Let your students see you struggle occasionally, let them see that you can't touch your toes in a pose. And it's okay—it gives them permission to not touch their toes.

❧ Lawyers, doctors, and yoga teachers

K: One of the things that inspired this book was my feeling that yoga teachers could really use advice from teachers who have gone down that path. I know that you have a new book coming out on the business of yoga, what was your inspiration for that?

D: I train teachers and there's lots of books on asana, but not a book out there about how you do the business of yoga. I've been teaching for twenty-two years. At some point, I recognized that to do this as a full time job, I had to treat it like a business. And it's not in my nature to do accounting or marketing. I just want to show up and teach and be like, "Namaste" [*he bows*]. That may be enough if you want to teach a class at the local gym, but if you want to make a career of it and really do it full time, you have to treat it like a business. A lawyer doesn't just show up that day at court, there's a lot of behind the scenes stuff. Doctors, they have all kinds of stuff that they have to do that doesn't have anything to do with examining a patient. I think we do ourselves and the next generation of yoga teachers a huge disservice if we don't teach them those skills.

K: Was there resistance for you to come to that place? As you said, you didn't want to be an accountant or business person…

D: When I was right out of college, I was okay with living on ramen noodles, you know, that type of lifestyle. But as you look into the crystal ball, and you see yourself maybe owning a home some day or having a family, or whatever your future aspirations might be, you start to think a little more. My aspirations are pretty humble, I don't want a mansion or a yacht or anything. I'm pretty content with a simple life, but I want a kid. And that involves having a home and health insurance and all kinds of stuff. And I don't want to sit at a desk all day, that's like my kryptonite. I want to teach yoga, and I think I'm good at it, but if I'm going to do that, it has to work for my future. If I'm going to lead a workshop or something, how can I market it? It doesn't have to be unethical. Marketing is just an invitation. It's unethical if you're lying. "I'll cure your cancer" or whatever. But if you're finding creative ways to invite people to take your class, it's unethical not to.

K: Why is it unethical not to?

D: If you think that what you're offering is truly of value, I don't have to twist your arm, I don't need to do a high-powered sales pitch. I take the view of "attraction" rather than the "promotion" side of things. If you sell quality product that fills a genuine need, people will want to buy it. You don't have to twist an arm or say "You're going to go to hell if you don't do my yoga class" or "You will never get laid!" or "Nobody will love you" or "God will kill a puppy." [*laughter*] I was raised Catholic, can you tell? There's a difference between capitalism and commercialism. Capitalism is supply and demand. The demand should already be there. The demand for food, for spirituality, health, wellness; these are all genuine needs that all human beings have. And if you can supply that, you don't have a problem because the needs are built-in. But what companies like Coca Cola or McDonald's do is say: "You don't really need this Big Mac or this Coke, but we're going to make you *think* that you need it." And that's incredibly expensive to do.

For a yoga teacher, the need is already there. People need their spirituality, their health, their need to feel good about themselves, to enjoy the experience of being human in their body. And we don't need to sell people on that, it's there. So all we have to do is get the attraction piece, to tell people that yoga helps with these things. And then provide the best class you can. Send the invitation. And enough people that resonate with your personality or teaching style, your unique skill set are going to find you and say, "Wow, I've been looking for someone who speaks my language, who understands me."

A friend of mine, she runs The Yoga Center of Minneapolis. She was very overweight, she tried everything and finally found yoga and took off the weight and kept it off. Now she teaches a yoga class called "Big Ass Yoga." It's for overweight women who don't feel comfortable going to your typical yoga class with all these hot skinny women with their little spaghetti strap tops and Lululemon pants and stuff. And it's packed. She can't teach enough classes to accommodate the women who want to take them. She's looking at the need, the insecure, overweight women who want to feel good in their bodies, and saying: "I welcome you, I support you, you're not going to feel judged here." I couldn't teach "Big Ass Yoga"

—I don't know what it is to be an overweight woman and struggle with that. But Jen does.

K: Where do you see the growth of yoga?

D: I will bet my life on this. That's how confident I am in this answer.

The next wave of yoga will be specialty yoga. By specialty, I mean speaking to the unique needs of groups. Maybe that's teaching Spanish language yoga, or Japanese. We live in a city with more Latinos and Asians than white people and we don't have any Asian language yoga classes or a Spanish yoga class. Does that make any sense at all? I have two people who've graduated from the Yoga Tree training who are sign language interpreters for the deaf community. I think that you're going to see a lot of people with either a special skill set, or somebody like Darcy Lyon, who's a psychologist and a yoga teacher, combining two things together. Or maybe personal experience: Les Leventhal deals with addiction, or Jen is dealing with her weight, or a battered wife who started to feel good about herself and her body. I can relate to that. I teach a lot of people with cancer in my restorative class and it's incredibly helpful to them. All of these things, people need more than what you can get from walking into a typical yoga class.

❧ Job vs. Profession?

K: Private yoga instruction is usually too expensive for most people, but the value that yoga teachers are providing is incredible. A student might take a class for $17 and it'll change their life. Do you think there might come a time when it'll be more like psychotherapy, where society will value it differently?

D: There's two schools of thought about yoga teaching...is it a job or is it a profession? I think there's a place for a person who wants to go teach at a gym, make a little money, get a free gym membership. There's nothing wrong with that; they're helping people, it's all good. But then there are those of us who see yoga as a profession. We need to start acting like professionals. And we have to ask ourselves things like: "Do you have a decent website?" Would you go to a doctor who had a website that looked like Charles Manson etched it onto a prison wall with a sharpened toothbrush or something? You wouldn't. You wouldn't go to a lawyer who had a website like that.

And professional ethics is another arena that's important. Would you go to a lawyer that wasn't giving 100% to all of his clients? Or "You're not as hot as my next client so I'm going to cut your time short"? Or confidentiality: "Yeah, come see me, it's great, but I'm going to tell everyone your stuff when I go for drinks with my buddies." You wouldn't go to that lawyer. And if it were found out that lawyer was doing that type of thing, we would very quickly disbar him. Because the profession as a whole has standards; it's not okay to break privilege. It's not okay to sleep with your clients, it's not okay to cheat or lie or promise things that are unrealistic, as has happened within the yoga community. Many teachers that we consider gurus have had scandals, really public stuff. And who then do we have to look up to? So I think we need to have some serious standards. If we want to be treated like therapists, instead of glorified aerobics instructors, we need to act like professionals. There needs to be consequences when one of us chooses to break those rules.

I'm not sitting here saying that I'm perfect or that I've never made a mistake. But there are serial perpetrators of these basic standards. We can all debate what brahmacharya means, but there are basic rules of ethical behavior that all professionals adhere to. Maybe a lawyer does it a little differently than a doctor, or than an accountant. But confidentiality, don't sleep with your students, don't make promises you can't keep, etc., this is basic stuff. So I don't take classes from teachers who aren't living the yamas and niyamas in a basic, basic way. Again, we can debate a lot of things, but we can agree that murder is wrong.

K: If you could only teach your teacher trainees only one thing, what would you that be?

D: That'd be hard! But I think it's respect. And that trickles in so many directions. If I'm respecting you when I'm touching or assisting you, you feel that. My assists are better. If I'm respecting you when I'm speaking to you (not, "that pose is terrible, what's *wrong* with you?"), you know it. I can adjust you, give you feedback, teach you a pose, teach you a breathing technique. There's self-respect. If we don't have enough self-respect to start and end our classes on time then...? Having yoga students is like having children in a way, that's part of the therapeutic relationship. They need structure and discipline and all of that. They need it in a loving, compassionate way. And so if you don't have self-respect, if you don't have respect for your students, you can do the best chaturanga or handstand in the world and it means absolutely nothing. And it bleeds through to everything else you do.

❦ The flatbed truck

K: Do you think what students expect today is different than it was 1000 years ago, or even 15 years ago?

D: I see several things. The good thing is, there are lots of people coming, they see value in yoga and standards are going up in many ways. If you were in India a thousand years ago, if you wanted to study with a guru, you'd have to beg them and they would say, "No." And you'd have to go back fifty times and then finally they would say "Ok." Here and now, it's almost like your ego and your bank account are rewarded by these having uber large classes. And that's not necessarily bad, but then we tend to do what the student demands as opposed to what the student needs.

Take, for example a hot sweaty class, nothing inherently wrong with that. But when you look at somebody's constitution, their doshas and stuff, what most fiery, crazy train-running-off-the-track Americans gravitate toward is what's comfortable. What they really need is to get quiet, maybe meditation or restorative class. But with the hot and sweaty, we're saying, "I'm going to give you more of the same." It's funny to do that.

I believe that the typical person, say you, for example, your life is a runaway train, and if you were to just jump off that train onto the meditation cushion, you'd get hurt or wouldn't be able to handle it. It'd be awful. It's just moving so fast. So I think of vinyasa yoga like a flatbed truck that pulls up next to the runaway train, so that you can step from the train to the truck. And then the truck slows down. So my vinyasa class starts off pretty fast-paced, matching the pace of your life, but by the end of class, I've slowed it down. So I've sort of tricked you into relaxation. But I think that most people, they crank up the heat, they do tons and tons of chaturangas and it makes people sweat and their arms shake and you hear students say that it was the best class ever. As if the translation for yoga is sweat.

As yoga teachers, we need to be looking at what our students need. And if you give your students what they need, you may lose a few students, because they may prefer someone who'll just run them through the wringer. For instance, I teach restorative yoga and I get some couch potatoes that come and really, what they need is a more active class. So I might tell them: "Hey, I hope you'll continue taking restorative class, it's really good for you. But you might consider also taking a gentle hatha class. Maybe not go straight to the Power Flow, but do something more active, you need to start moving some energy." Let's look at each student as a unique individual and ask what they need, as opposed to what they demand. The teacher should be running the class, not the student.

❧ Go with your passion

K: What were the first few years of teaching like?

D: It's such a different animal now! When I started teaching, there were like three teaching training programs in the country. I wound up at Kripalu. It wasn't like there was a Yoga Alliance or yoga studios or anything like that. When you were the most experienced student in the room and your teacher had to go on vacation, they'd say you were teaching Tuesday night's class. And you were like: "Doh! Ah!!!" And then you do that a few times and if you liked it, you might go to the ashram for a while. It was really different. Most people started out of their living room. I'd have a little class with five students. And you thought were you a rock star with those five students a few nights a week. And all of a sudden there was Sri Madonna and Ricky Martin, and Jane Fonda was quoted as saying that if she'd known about yoga she would've never done aerobics. And then there were people pouring into yoga classes because Sting could have a prolonged orgasm or something. All of a sudden, I was a "Yoga Teacher" and most people didn't even know what yoga was, except for some weird thing where you put your foot behind your head. I went from five to ten to thirty or forty people. It felt like almost overnight.

But if I were starting out today, I'd probably start with the gym. It's a good place to start. Some of my best students came from gyms. The students are a little less discerning and it's a great way to create a following, make some money, and get some teaching experience. So when you go to a studio, you can say that you have this mailing list or maybe they'd have heard of you before. That's be my advice, start with the gym or your living room with a few friends. Better yet, go volunteer. Go to the battered women's shelter, the homeless shelter, or to a hospice and teach people breathing techniques. Whatever it is that you feel passionate about, go do it. Go to the drug rehab!

❧ Lessons from Mozart

K: I've talked to some teachers who think that if you haven't studied seriously for at least ten years and taught informally for another ten years, you have no business teaching yoga. What do you think about that?

D: I don't buy that. I don't need to go to Mozart to learn how to play the piano. It'd be nice, but the person that I need to go to who can teach me something about the piano is the person who knows more about the piano than I do. I do think it's good to have a healthy respect for your limits. Cranking you deep into a pose is not a good idea if I don't know what I'm doing. And I think a lot of new teachers should avoid that. They should use verbal assists and press points. And really simple, gentle assists. You know what I mean? Having a healthy respect for where you're at as a teacher and some humility is really important, and that said, how are you ever going to become a teacher unless you get out there and teach? It's like being a tattoo artist, at some point you're tattooing something permanent on someone's skin and the only way you can get good at it is to do it. Hopefully you don't spell their mother's name wrong.

❧ You're the bell, not the dog food

K: If there was one thing that you wish someone would've told you when you started, what would that be?

D: I think it would be "You're the bell, not the dog food." You know Pavlov's dog? How he hears the bell and he salivates because he associates the bell with the food? People come to my class in varying degrees of discomfort: emotional, mental or physical. They do the practice, they feel better. And I happen to be present for that. It's the yoga that's doing it, just like the dog food that's satisfying the dog. And yet, the dog starts to think that it's the bell that's satisfying him. This is completely natural for the dog to do, but for the bell to think, "I'm dog food" is just insanity. And yet, that's what we often do as yoga teachers. We get wrapped up in these people coming to class saying, "Oh my God, you're so great, you changed my life, you're amazing. Let me bow at your lotus feet." But I didn't do anything. All I did was hold the space in which you could experience yoga. Nothing more, nothing less. It's an important role, I don't want to diminish it. At the same time, don't give yourself too much credit. Yoga's been around for thousands of years and it'll be around for thousands of years after you're gone.

Yes, people are going to throw themselves at your feet because they'll be so grateful that they were suffering and now they're suffering a lot less. And they're going to associate you with that healing, but it wasn't you, it was the yoga. Have respect for the practice. And for the long lineage, of guru to disciple who turns into the guru. Teacher, student, teacher, student. Hopefully, you'll inspire somebody who goes on and adds their unique voice and their unique personality to the mix and yoga will evolve again. It's really not about you, it's about them, it's about the practice. You really start to believe the bullshit in the beginning. And it is bullshit. We all like to be told how great we are, it's human nature. But you've got to have a mindful awareness of where that's coming from.

❧ Live in yoga

K: One of the things I was really struck by in your book, *Yoga and the Path of the Urban Mystic,* was "I'm torn by living a deeply contemplative life and being a full-fledged member of my secular community." How do you feel like you've been able to reconcile those things?

D: My whole concept of the "urban mystic" isn't really new.

Jack Kornfield wrote a book, *After the Ecstasy: The Laundry.*
Different authors have addressed this in different ways. To go
live in a monastery or a cave is fine, if that's your dharma. But
it's not mine. And everything you do should be a yoga
practice. If you think of asana as movement of the body, and
pranayama as breathing, you've been doing vinyasa since
before you got out of the womb. And you will continue that
one movement as it's led to the next to the next to the next
until movement stops at death. The difference between what
99.9% of people are doing and what a yogi is doing is that a
yogi tries to do these things consciously. I try to move
consciously as much as possible, whether it's my actions on
the yoga mat or in the world. With that in mind, every action,
whether it's making dinner, the act of driving my car, of raising
my son, of making love, is yoga. And always having
permission to forget. You wouldn't ask someone to sit and
meditate and *never* forget to repeat their mantra. Or never
forget to watch their breath. You'd never ask one of your
students to do a pose perfectly every time, to never fall out of
tree pose. I'm going to come to tree pose and fall out, come
to tree and fall out. Over time, you fall out less and less, life is
like that.

For more about Darren,
visit www.DarrenMain.com

❦ CHAPTER 6

GEOFFREY RONIGER

Geoffrey Roniger has become well known for his unique approach to yoga. It emphasizes sound biomechanical alignment principles, intuitive movement, and eloquent use of metaphor to translate this ancient tradition into our contemporary cultural vernacular. He graduated from Vanderbilt University with a degree in European Studies in 1998. After traveling to Edinburgh, Scotland to renovate a 19th century church, he returned to the United States where he graduated from Piedmont Yoga Studio's 18-month Advanced Studies Program, and formally apprenticed with Richard Rosen and Rodney Yee.

Geoffrey was the on-site yoga teacher for Salesforce.com, Amyris Biotechnologies, Beverly Prior Architects, Juice Design, and Urban Revision. Through this experience he created "Workplace Wellness", an effective and accessible program that uses modified yoga techniques to counteract the negative effects of sitting all day at a desk. Geoffrey's private clientele has included several CEOs dealing with high levels of stress, members of the New Orleans Hornets looking to rehabilitate and restore their bodies, and health care professionals searching for a reliable method of self-care. Geoffrey has served on the teacher training staff at The Yoga Loft in San Francisco since 2006, and he leads regular workshops and retreats. He volunteered for Urban Zen events at both "V Day" in New Orleans and the Special Olympics, successfully implementing therapeutic yoga techniques for evacuees of Hurricane Katrina and athletes with disabilities. He was then appointed to their faculty for Urban Zen's Integrative Therapy Program in New York. Geoffrey has been featured in the "Awakened Athletes", "Masterclass", and "Basics columns" for Yoga Journal as well as in the Gaiam video, Yoga Now. He returned to his hometown of New Orleans where he lives with his wife, two sons and two dogs. Geoffrey is the founder of and primary teacher at Freret Street Yoga, in New Orleans, which he opened as a community resource for the promotion of the practice that he so passionately loves.

———∿∿∿———

Talking to Geoffrey Roniger makes you want to settle into yourself and find a soft place to land in your practice. While extremely thoughtful and eloquent in his speech, he's also hilarious and will swear like a pirate when the occasion calls for it. Geoffrey speaks so fondly of his students, you realize very quickly that he's committed to fostering growth and intimacy through the student/teacher relationship. His humility is inviting and makes you want to listen harder, because you might miss something if you're not truly present for the conversation.

❧ An embodied example

Karen: How did you decide to be a yoga teacher?

Geoffrey: I had a sort of mid-life crisis when I was 23. I was living in Edinburgh, Scotland, and I was helping to renovate a 19th century church into this amazing Ashtanga studio. I was taking yoga classes from the most amazing teachers and seeing that it was possible to start your own thing because Nick Loening, the guy who was starting the center, was just such a character, and he was doing it. He'd been a sailor for Greenpeace for a long time and had this vision of what this church *could* be and was like "screw it" and decided to make it happen. He was an embodied example of what it's like to just live a lifestyle that works for you, that's an expression of yourself. So I got quiet with *myself* and asked what I would do if money didn't exist and the only thing that I could come up with was that I just wanted to keep studying yoga, because I was that in love with it.

Even when I moved to San Francisco and started studying with Rodney Yee and Richard Rosen, I was like: "Dude, I would love to teach this", but I kept thinking that I was too young–I was only 24 or 25 at the time. So when I did my teacher training program, it was just to have an immersion course, not to teach. But then Jane Dobson came to class and told me that she was starting a studio and "you have to be a part of it, you've got something to offer." I was thinking: "No, no, I'm not ready, I'm still studying…." But Jane just got me to try it. So I feel like I got duped into teaching [*laughing*] because it was not at all what I was intending.

At first it was like, one person or two people would come to class. And I was like: "This isn't working." And I was still waiting tables at Rose's Café. And then somehow I got referred my first private client. It was from a teacher who was traveling for six weeks and asked if I could teach his private client. It was $100 an hour. And I was teaching her twice a week. She and I really hit it off. And I was like, "Oh my God! I could earn $100 an hour teaching this woman who's so grateful instead of running around in a restaurant like a chicken with the head cut off. Whoa, what kind of thing is this?!" So I started getting referrals from friends and friends of friends, and I just had this handful of privates that I was teaching, along with my public classes.

But what really tipped the scales for me was when Tony Sanchez, who I had waited on every Wednesday morning for years, told me that he was closing his yoga studio and moving to Baja Mexico. He had this corporate group that was he was teaching a couple times a week and would I be interested? They were paying $250 each time I would teach them. And I was like, "Uh…yeah!" And that was the game changer. Right then, I quit my waitering job. So it was a lot of luck and kind of "in spite of myself" because I would say that I was very shy about promoting myself or trying to get myself out there in the beginning.

❧ Workplace wellness

K: As you say, you sort of fell into it, but teaching in the corporate workplace or as you call it, "Workplace Wellness," has become a really big part of what you do.

G: I started seeing at the time that this population was different than any of the other people that I was teaching. They had common needs. And I started to design and refine specific sequences that seemed to alleviate symptoms of back pain and neck pain that they were having. And not only that, I took the kind of high strung, stressed out energy that they were showing up to class with, and I was able to help them, somehow, transmute it into a calmer place by the time they left.

Then I started to get to know them personally. I could joke around with them and get to know them as human beings–not that I don't do that with public classes–but it was like the armor was coming down. They were seeing yoga in a way that maybe their pre-conceptions of it would have previously stopped them. It was like a Judo trick that got them to do it. Yoga touches you in a way that's personal and it's going to meet you where you are, and it's going to avail itself to you; the spiritual aspect of it. And it was really sweet that it was happening in this corporate space. It was full-on fluorescent lights, tables, computer humming in the background. On the surface, it was so incongruous with what we associate with yoga, but seeing it happen in that setting, I realized that this is powerful and effective and why in the hell aren't other companies using the same service?

Then it was like a light bulb went off and I started reaching out by sending out mailers of "Hey, this is how yoga will benefit you." I had hundreds of doors closed in my face but then several doors opened and invited me in. It was really cool to see how effective yoga was as another form of team-building for groups. When people are in an embodied place, they're calmer and more receptive. It was sweet, and I continued to experiment. I have some go-to recipes, but I feel like I'm always learning from students and trying to refine how I serve that population.

~ Bridging old and new

K: On the Freret Street Yoga website, you write "We fundamentally believe that yoga is a living tradition that should evolve to meet the demands of our modern culture. While we pay homage to the source of this great practice and to all of the teachers who have transmitted its essence through the years, we think that yoga should continue to serve humanity rather than be *preserved* as a historical artifact." It sounds like you're trying to bridge something...

G: Yeah, it's a bridge. I just got to a point where I kept thinking we would go to India but didn't. I had this sort of nagging voice in my head that said that I can't call myself a yoga practitioner because I hadn't made my pilgrimage to India or I haven't studied with those gurus or at least seen the place where it came from. But shit man, I pay attention to my breath and I wake up early to stand on my head for 10 minutes at a time. And I read the old scriptures and study them earnestly.

I was in the Czech Republic during college and in the middle of a square in Prague, there was this Dixieland jazz band. Czech people playing big 'ole New Orleans tunes on their horns. And all the things they were playing were things I'd grown up with. If I was being a snob, I would've been like "This isn't 'real' Dixieland jazz, they've probably never even been to New Orleans." But how snobbish is that! And how inaccurate, because the sounds that were coming from their lungs through the vibration of their horns was as joyful and as rhythmic as anything that I'd heard as a kid. The experience was really parallel to my experience as a yoga practitioner because it's a living thing that we do every time we come to the mat.

Every time we come to the mat, it's different. If we can remember that we can have the same spirit that they originally did, it's an honest exploration. We have to navigate our own internal landscape, maybe embody the same pioneering spirit that BKS Iyengar had, to figure out the truth for himself, to really know, to grapple with these postural configurations that were challenging for him. If we're going to make yoga viable, we have to consider ourselves practitioners of it instead of snobbish historical preservationists. We can't be throwing out all the work that they've done, we don't need to reinvent the wheel, but they've paved the way and we can walk that road for ourselves. Yoga is getting so popular in Japan and China, and different parts of Europe. We're all part of this universal quest to discover and know what yoga is for ourselves.

❧ Lead with your heart

K: What's the best advice you've ever gotten?

G: It'd have to be "Teach with your heart and not with your head." I make that mistake, all too often, of trying to teach something that I'm still working out on my own or trying to understand and I get too cerebral or insecure about whether or not someone else is enjoying it. But somehow, if I can connect back with my heart, then the same information will come out in a way that lands more easily on the student. I love what Rodney said one time, "it's got nothing to do with what you're saying, it has everything to do with the vibration of your voice." And that really struck a chord with me. It's the vibration of your voice and what's coming from you as an embodied creature that ultimately penetrates into someone else. Not about your anatomical knowledge or your clever sequence or your interesting musings on an obscure yoga sutra. It always comes back to the vibrational quality of your voice. I love that piece of advice.

K: What would you say to a student who's thinking about becoming a teacher?

G: Trust your practice. Bottom line, trust your practice and let it guide you. Because if you don't, you'll always feel like you need more trainings, that you don't know enough, that someone has an approach that's more effective than yours, and you'll start to get away from what you intuitively know. If you put all the trust into your practice and teach from there, it doesn't matter if you're teaching at a high profile studio, a free community clinic, or a low profile gym, your teaching will be more rewarding, more satisfying and more thoroughly received by people.

❧ The ecology of the body

K: You've been teaching the New Orleans Hornets, right? I imagine you're having to do a little translation of yoga for them, right?

G: Oh my God, I'm having so much fun trying to figure out how to modify poses for men who are seven feet tall. How am I'm going to position them in the room so that they don't hit their hands on the ceiling fans? And how am I going to get them into a different frame of mind where self-competition and the motto "No pain, no gain"—or that they have to push harder to get results—where they understand those things don't actually work? This is a different way of being in yourself and with yourself. They keep coming back and are loving it so much. According to them, what's *not* emphasized in professional athletic training is recovery, restoration, and prevention. They're getting that if their body is more aligned and they're using certain joints properly, their chances of avoiding injury is greater. To them, it translates into longer contracts and more money. But they also want to be able to enjoy their family when they're done with their basketball career, instead of being plagued by back pain, unable to run or even walk in the park with their kids. So they're getting long-term sustainability within the ecology of the body. That's going to be the next wave of athletic training. It's funny, that yoga is the "cutting edge" thing. I always get a chuckle out of explaining that these "new" techniques are actually way way old techniques.

❧ Elation on a woman's face

K: The work you've done with Urban Zen Project is really fascinating. Can you tell us a little about that?

G: The Urban Zen Project that Donna Karan started, and my teacher Rodney Yee is the director of, is a phenomenal service to the world. I'm honored to be a part of it. It's great to see  how it's been way more codified and systematized in terms of how to help hospital patients, and how we can use it as a template for other situations like the Special Olympics event. Basically, it's making the simplest practices out of what they're calling "in bed movements," or movements that anybody can do when they're in a supine position.

I trailed an integrative therapist in New York and followed her through the hospital cancer ward to see what they did. I saw the elation on a woman's face who looked *so* down trodden when we walked into her room. But then five minutes of doing her "sun salutations"–which was just her raising her arms, not even to shoulder level, but raising and lowering them in synch with her breath–and she looked totally different. It was such a tender thing to observe and so powerful because you realize that you don't have to be in a certain physical shape to do this, you don't have to have a spiritual slant to benefit from this. You, as a human being, can try some of these "yoga experiments" and find more energy within yourself, less stress and hopefully can reconnect with your truer state of contentment, even in the face of great difficulty.

We taught 5,000 women who were bussed in by Oprah to the Superdome for a Post-Katrina Urban Zen event.[3] Some of them would just get into supported corpse pose, basically savasana with an open chest. They would get out of ten minutes of conscious breathing and look at me like: "Whoa! What is this thing? I've never felt so clear in my body." And I was like: "Well, I guess we call it yoga." And they would be shocked and like: "No way! I thought yoga was standing on your head or putting your leg behind your head or something." I just find it so incredibly gratifying to teach yoga to people who would ordinarily never try it. And to let them know what it isn't. To just demystify it and translate it to them. I've always been inspired by it and always feel like we mutually energize each other when we do that.

For more about Geoffrey,
visit www.FreretStreetYoga.com

---

[3] Geoffrey participated in Eve Ensler's inspiring Superlove event held at the Superdome April 11th & 12th, 2008. At the event, Urban Zen Foundation hosted a Well-Being Sanctuary, where women had their minds relaxed, bodies touched through yoga, massage and aromatherapy, and spirits uplifted through love.

ॐ CHAPTER 7

JASON NEMER

Jason Nemer sees himself as blessed with countless teachers on his path. His younger brother brought him into gymnastics. This is when his "inverted" career started, in 1987. Jason's teenage years were deeply influenced by the training techniques of Russian and Bulgarian Acrobatic Masters. Competing among the best acrobats in the world opened his eyes to many advanced expressions of body control and balance. Jason was a two-time US Jr. National Champion in partner acrobatics, and represented the US at the World Championships in 1991 in Beijing. In 1996, he performed acrobatics in the Opening Ceremonies at the Olympic games. *Yoga came to him in the last semester of university. After that first class there was no looking back. Connection to the breath and the lifestyle philosophy of yoga filled him with so much joy. His world was changed, and only continues to get more rich with the wisdom of daily yogic practices. Currently, Jason trains in Acrobatics with Master Lu Yi at the Circus Center in San Francisco. Scott Blossom is his teacher of Ayurveda & Asana. Sianna Sherman shows him how poetic grace in motion can be. He studies bodywork with the Thai Massage Circus and privately with the Metta Mama Jenn Yarro. Jason feels blessed to be sharing this practice with the world and will continue to develop himself and AcroYoga as his dharma.*

—◦◦◦—

Jason and I met early in the morning at a friend's apartment where he was staying for a week before he was off to more global travels. He invited me to sit with him on his BioMat, an amethyst filled mat that sends negative ions through the body. He said that it's one of his secrets of self-care, allowing him to maintain his crazy traveling schedule. As I sipped the delicious tea that Jason brewed for us, I was struck by how grounded and soft his energy was. After having seen him in so many high-flying acrobatic partnering poses, it was wonderful to see that he's a land animal too. Although as we talked, I frequently felt the urge to go upside down, but I managed to stay right side up during our interview!

❧ Trading stocks

Karen: How did you come to be a yoga teacher?

Jason: I was at UC San Diego, finishing up my undergrad degree in Economics. That last semester, I took a class on Asian philosophy and my first yoga class, Hatha Yoga. And the yoga class was at 7am and I would roll out of bed at like 6:55, look at my clock and think, "There's no way I can go to yoga today." So I would usually stroll in for that hour-long yoga class fifteen minutes late, but I would get done with class and I would feel *so* good. And that put all my economic interest—I was going to be a stock trader [*we laugh*]—that's what I thought I was going to do…I put all that on hold and pushed me in a different direction.

The summer following my graduation, I took three months to read a ton of books and I started practicing different styles of yoga. I didn't know where it was going to lead me, but I knew that I wasn't going to be a stock trader. I had tons of questions and a big thirst to learn about yoga. I never stopped learning and eventually started doing teacher trainings, getting out into the world and started teaching.

K: Do you feel like it was a conscious decision? Or were you just following something?

J: Well, I've been teaching gymnastics and acrobatics since I was a kid so I knew how to teach movement arts. And yoga has a lot of similarities and a lot of big differences from those things. So I feel like I was already equipped to look at bodies, to help people through fear. I had a lot of the skill set already there so it was really just finding ways to blend it with this new knowledge base that I didn't know much about. So I had to learn it, embody it first, and then get the confidence to share it.

❧ There was this girl

K: You've helped to create a new form of yoga, did you set out to do that? Did it happen organically?

J: It was super organic. I got out of Bikram teacher training and was living in Sacramento and San Francisco, just trying to make it as a yoga teacher and I kept hearing about this girl named "Jenny" [Sauer-Klein, now co-founder of AcroYoga,] through mutual friends. She was training in circus arts and a yoga teacher, and people just thought we should meet. Once we finally met, we jammed—and I know traditional acrobatics and she knows more of the therapeutic partner yoga stuff. So we did an exchange and were up until five in the morning talking about this practice that could incorporate partner inversions and how that would build the trust and you could do partner stretching to open up the body and this therapeutic yoga stuff with partners could be the foundation for higher level acrobatics, etc. We envisioned everything except the

 Thai massage piece that first night. We started teaching a few weeks after that.

It was really quite cosmic, being that we're here in the Bay and we would go to Dolores Park—that was our office—and just jammed a lot. Through our jamming, we had maybe three to six months of jamming and teaching and were like: "Wow, we have a lot of material, what should we do? Maybe put a book together?" And we started crafting the book and once we had the book, we started feeling like: "Well, maybe instead of just making a book, maybe we should teach people how to teach this." So it was really gradual, step-by-step and thought out. It started out with inspiration and passion, then there were a lot of deliberate steps to get things to where they are now.

K: Did you find it hard to bring it to studios?

J: We got really lucky. The first studio we came to was Yoga Tree [in San Francisco] and the owner, Tim Dale's parents were acrobats so he loved it and was super open to it. Our first workshop was a Valentine Day's workshop and we had 35 people. So right from the beginning, we've had a lot of support and success.

There are definitely studios or certain styles of yoga that are less...I don't think I've ever taught AcroYoga at an Iyengar institute [*laughter*]. That's is actually funny because a lot of what we do is passive release work, which you could do on a block or a bolster, or you could do it over someone's feet. And I think that the days of feeling like we can only go to Power Yoga studios are starting to shift as our offerings have expanded. What we've done over the years is that we've gotten really clear on how our offerings can support what people are already doing in their studios. And then eventually, if they're really interested in what the full practice is, they'll seek us out.

❧ Nervousness = Divine Shakti

K: What were your first years of teaching like? Were there really hard moments? Really great moments?

J: A lot of both. I had a friend who's an acrobat that I trained with for years, and I was telling him how nervous I was to

teach yoga and he didn't understand at all. I would have to take a lot of deep breaths before I could go on and teach for the first couple of months. He didn't understand it and I couldn't explain it to him until I really started to understand what was happening. I think that nervousness, or nervous energy is actually channeling divine shakti and when you're doing something that pushes you to your edge, it's like, growth is

there because you have this new energy that's entering your body. So what I felt that was so different between yoga and acrobatics, was that acrobatics is not a spiritual practice. It can be, anything can. Drinking tea can be a spiritual practice if you have that intention and that ability to bring it to that. But intrinsically, teaching yoga is so much about opening people and connecting them to their sweet essence, so I was really reverent of the process of bringing people to that. So the hard moments were just stepping into that very sweet vulnerable state that people get to when they do yoga. The amazing moments were all over the place. Being able to travel the world and share this practice, many of these practices, has been really cool. [*laughs*]

❧ Only as deep as the teachers

K: As a whole, where do you think yoga is, in the US? In the World?

J: It's really different in different places. I just went to South America to teach, and over the past couple of years, it's the first place in the world where I've seen and felt yoga on the decline. Because everywhere else I've been, previous to Brazil, has just been growing, growing, growing. I think the US is one of the leading places in the world—in my humble and biased opinion. Europe has really caught up a lot, I've been teaching in Europe for maybe five years. The practitioners, especially in the UK and Spain, they're really starting to come into their intermediate level of practice, and definitely advanced in some places.

I think what's really exciting for me is to see people who've practiced now for five to ten years, because it can be a fad for some people for maybe six months or a year. But if people really stick with the practice for five to ten years, the types of shifts that it produces is really palpable and tangible.

Asia's another interesting place. I was just at the Asia Yoga Conference. I went to the first and second year and it was really difficult because they didn't understand yoga *or* English. [*I'm laughing*] To try and teach them yoga in the English language was *really* challenging. You can't have a translator because you have Korean, Japanese, Thai, and three different Chinese dialects! That was part of the reason that I didn't go back for three years, it was really far and really challenging. But when I went back this year, I was really impressed to see that the level of yoga, and English, it's all really growing. A lot of yoga taught in Asia is actually now taught in English.

What I think happened in Brazil–I've talked to a couple of friends and there's a friend who wrote an article about it–I think that if you don't have teachers who have deep roots, they can't take students to a deep place. So if somebody goes to a weekend teacher training, or even a week-long, or month-long training, then they bring it back, their students can get inspired to a certain level, but if there's not enough depth in the teachers, the community's not going to grow that deep. Also, in Brazil, there's a strong pleasure culture and yoga will bring you up into your edges and make you confront things. You know, they just love to have a good time. There are some other reasons too. Like the Brazilians are already so connected to spirit and their body, I don't feel like they need it as much as a lot of other cultures because they already have their ways to connect to spirit. But I'm also excited to continue to invest in South America because there's no place that yoga can't be a blessing and a benefit.

❧ Do it for your students

K: What's your relationship to technology like?

J: I was one of the last humans to join Facebook. I think I joined Facebook about four months ago. [*we're laughing*] I was like: "No, I do enough on the computer, I don't want to have recreation time on the computer too." But one of my friends, Kasey Luber, said, "Jason don't do Facebook for *you*, do it for all the AcroYoga teachers and all of your students." And I was like, "Ah, I can't argue with that! Shit! I'm going to have to do it, aren't I?"

My relationship with technology is growing, I feel. I watched the Facebook movie on an airplane recently and I was really moved. I was really amazed that one good idea has connected the whole world in such a beautiful way. Google too. There's a lot of amazing technologies that are connecting the world and the more that it grows, the more the desire for people to have physical connection and real-time community grows. And I feel like AcroYoga is the answer to Facebook and Google, in a way. And they all support the same goal–people don't want to be alone. And the more that people spend time in cyber-land, they get a certain sense of connection, but they don't get deeply satisfied, so I feel like they're complimentary technologies. The technology of cyber-land and the technology of getting together in the park and playing and talking to people. I'm using my technology as a vehicle to get back to the roots of why the other technologies were designed: to connect people.

❧ The Source

K: What do you think about the student/teacher relationship nowadays, as opposed to maybe in India, "back in the day"?

J: I think that there are a lot of essential levels that are the same. Finding a teacher is finding someone who has been there and done things that you haven't done yet. So in the absence of your own experiential knowledge, you surrender to the teacher and you are therefore able to learn a lot faster because you're not having to learn all of your wisdom, you're taking on their wisdom as your own. As that process goes along, you still check in with your own bodily wisdom. So I feel like surrendering to a teacher and taking on their wisdom is a really sacred act, and whether it was 10,000 years ago, 5,000 years ago, or now, that part is the same.

What's different is that now we get on airplanes, we fly around, and we meet thousands of people. The amount of knowledge that we have at our fingertips with the internet— gives us so much more accessibility to faster downloads. But faster doesn't mean better or deeper.

If I was living in Pune a long time ago, if I wanted to go to the next village, then I'm either walking, or riding whatever animal they were riding in Pune! My availability to multiple inputs would be less. And I also feel that there's something to be said about finding one guru, but that's where things have shifted a lot. I've definitely found that lots of teachers have influenced me.

I think there are multiple teachers for multiple periods of your life and I feel that I've literally had hundreds of teachers over the past twenty-six years that I've been studying movement arts and all these things. I feel that each teacher kind of leads me to the next. Daniel Tucker—one of my music teachers— has led me to my ability to access my own bhakti. Until I found Jai [Uttal], Daniel Paul, and Daniel Tucker, I'd have to go to yoga classes to access this feeling of bhakti, of singing. But when I studied with them enough, I learned to self-source that.

That's another way that it's been the same for eons: when you find a good teacher, they turn your attention back into yourself as your source of inspiration. There are differences but there are some age-old things that will always be the same.

❧ Leave the negative

K: If there was one thing you wish someone would've told you when you started this journey, what would that be?

J: I don't know. I feel like everything that I've experienced so far has been so beautiful that I couldn't imagine having any one thing steer in a direction that's better than what I've experienced. My mom's been a really influential person in my life and she's always encouraged me to just follow my dreams and to go for it. That is the thing that she has supported in me and that was probably one of the biggest things for me, whereas there's been other parental figures and people in my life that made me feel like there were limits to what I could do; because you *should* do things a certain way. My mom's always encouraged me to just follow my dreams and that's one of the biggest reasons that I'm here now.

K: What's the best advice you've ever gotten?

J: One thing that I got when I was sixteen from this amazing gymnastics coach was: "Get the negative people out of your life." I've juggled that, you know, "yogically," because there's a question of how much growth there can be when there are people that cause challenge. But I feel that to a large degree, I've been able to surround myself with amazing people who inspire me. There's no way to not have difficult situations but I don't surround myself with an intimate crew where I might have multiple difficult situations. I really have been blessed to be surrounded by people who are really supportive, really sweet, and challenge me in ways that are productive for my growth.

❧ Clarity as an anthem

K: What would you say to a student who's thinking of becoming a teacher?

J: Go for it! This is something I heard years ago: "Take ten years to become a student before you're a teacher, and then take another ten years to teach before you teach teachers." So I feel like, if you want to be a teacher, it's because you're dedicated to this path that you're on, you're not worried about when it's going to turn into a lifestyle that's going to be productive for you financially, or all those other reasons.

Going back, one of the harder things that's also been a blessing was having to really commit to the yoga path. When I first started, I was living in my van in San Francisco trying to make it as a yoga teacher. I could've gotten a restaurant job so things were easier, but I really dedicated myself to just yoga and in doing that, I didn't have extra money, so I didn't have extra distractions. I was either eating, sleeping, doing yoga, or talking about yoga. So that was a challenging and beneficial thing.

And another good piece of advice that I got was: "Evaluate your yoga practice once every fourteen years." So often, students will be checking their asana, asking how their hanumanasana is, or whatever. If we really give ourselves a *long* time to steep in the practice, I think that it can be a much more beneficial way to interact with it. Instead of having a check list or having a timeline. Just knowing this is something that we'll be doing for the rest of our lives, letting the timeline expand can create more space for really appreciating the journey.

There's no finish line. That's what's great about the practice too. There's never going to be a point where you'll be totally fluent in yoga and you'll have to find another practice. There's no end to how many ways we can see harmony and balance and beauty in all aspects of our life coming together. Being that there's no finish line, rushing or going slow really depends on where you want to get with your practice–and that's a lifelong question.

K: Is there anything else you want to offer here?

J: For up-and-coming teachers or yogis: Be clear about what you want in your life. I had a number of years where "Clarity" was my anthem. If you're clear, you'll call it in. Clarity is the first step. Willpower is something that some people have more or less of, but if you have all the willpower in the world, but you don't have clarity, you're going to just spin in so many directions. A lot of the people that are in the deepest amount of suffering are the people who are disconnected to what they truly want, and who don't know what they can truly offer. So really clarify what your goals are, what you want to offer the world. It can take a number of years, and it's always a moving target, but without clarity, people really get stuck in a cycle that doesn't serve them or the world. I would start there and try to never lose sight of the belief that it can be easy, it can be good, it can be beautiful. And there are so many examples of people around the world who are living that way.

For more about Jason,
visit www.AcroYoga.org

❧ CHAPTER 8

DUNCAN WONG

Master Duncan Wong is the creator of the Yogic Arts™ system. It is an organic movement technology that synthesizes the stillness and simplicity of Zen philosophy with comprehensive core dynamic flow mechanics. The system blends mixed martial arts, mudra, and stance structure, interdisciplinary bodywork therapy, and a refined approach to assisting and alignment. He infuses it all with the rhythm of modern dance and urban breakbeats.

Duncan has the ability to multi-assist the entirety of a pose. He is able to convey the essential relationship between each posture and their intrinsically interconnected fluidity. This attunes our minds and hearts to this ancient wisdom technology of the mystery schools. He feels that this is the best method for mirroring our own life movement and lifestyle choices; to awaken the insight necessary to realize our destiny.

Yogic Arts is, according to Duncan, a personal investigation of the ways in which we relate to the primal movements of all wisdom cultures. It emphasizes contact, connection and alignment of elemental and energetic spiritual forms. At its most immediate level, Yogic Arts is advanced technique experienced in a comprehensive and compassionate style.

—~∽w∽~—

Master Wong and I connected at a very transformative time in his life, just as he was about to become the father to twin boys. We had a long conversation from Japan, where he makes his home. It seemed that imminent fatherhood was a catalyst for reflection on his life, his career and the future of his family life. Change was in the air and maybe even more than usual, Duncan was contemplative and in touch with the larger aspects of yogic life. Duncan is a wonderful mixture of humor, vibrancy and wisdom. Just like Yogic Arts, our conversation flowed from one thing to the next, neither of us knowing where we would end up.

❧ Washing dishes

Karen: How did you come to decide to be a yoga teacher?

Duncan: I want to preface this by saying that all my answers will be clichés [*we laugh*]. Because clichés are sometimes true. But on being a yoga teacher, I feel like my whole life prepared me for this position. I'm a yogi who believes in reincarnation and even group reincarnation. I feel like this is what I've been doing for a long time, my practice has helped me recall that it's been longer than my life span. With something that feels so right, it's a little too natural to be just within this lifetime.

I left my home in San Francisco at a very young age, at about eleven, and I was a child laborer. I did construction, washed dishes, worked in a kitchen, painting, anything basically. Looking back, I realize that I was just a kid, but back then, we thought we were cool. We were running around with motorcycle gangs and living in artist communes. So we thought we were really cool and I always played a game with myself. I started teaching when I was eighteen, I was *so* young, but I would say to myself, "Well, let's just say that if this doesn't work out, I can always go back to being a laborer. I can always go back to washing dishes or digging ditches. But let's see where this goes." And it just kept going and going and 25 years later, it's still going. I'm more inspired and I wash dishes at home and I do miss labor work sometimes but I go hiking instead [*laughs*]. It's been going well.

Photo: Minoru Nitta (www.jetsets.jp)

❧ Like Yoda

K: What were the first few years like?

D: I wouldn't say I was struggling...but I was taking my position as a teacher, taking my seat as a sensei, as it were. So I felt more like an equal, and it was overwhelming, but a great challenge and it helped me to rise to the occasion and recognize the distinction between teacher and student. And yet, of course, we're all equal. But there is responsibility and that took years to understand.

First and foremost, was the dual-edge-sword of safe power. I had to figure out how to protect people physically and emotionally. I mean, guru status is a really daunting position for us to hold. People turn to us like Yoda and think that you have all the answers because you're a yoga teacher. So you take on the responsibility of learning. Maybe because I project my "super-hero archetype" or something, but people have always called me "Master" or "Young Master" since I was really young. And they'd ask me a lot of heavy questions about the universe and life, about relationships and destiny. So I had to take on that role. I've had a lot of intense training, I've studied martial arts, yoga, and massage, all to a certain level over the last few decades and I've synthesized it together. I call it my "Triple PhD," even though I never went to school [*we laugh*]. It requires a lot of contemplation and research and practice to formulate responses for your students. That's one of the responsibilities, to have real answers that are experiential.

K: Can you remember a really exhilarating moment during those first few years?

D: Absolutely! Just being in the room, taking on how to "Om" and embodying that. And to be unapologetically spiritual, as my original yoga parents, the Jivamukti masters, Sharon Gannon and David Life, would say. Just "om-ing" and feeling the resonant frequency of people feeling it too. And the feeling of accomplishment for holding a space where people can feel a transformation of some kind; that is a powerful responsibility and very exhilarating. Like it's bigger than us. That's always been exciting.

❧ Coming full circle

K: Where do you think yoga is in its growth?

D: Infantile. I think it's really early. I think that the survival of our species, and for us to thrive as a planetary, or inter-planetary community requires us to use the other 80–90% of our brain and take it to the next dimension, not to sound too far out or anything. But I think there's a lot of growth for humanity and for yoga in general. I think yoga, if you want to use the term yoga, is one of the keystones, or portals to access higher realms of interconnectivity. It's how we can just connect instantly in a generous way and move beyond the greed mentality that's brought us to the brink of disaster here environmentally and socially. I think there's a global collective consciousness shift and it's very exciting. But it's going to take motivation, it's going to

Photo: Minoru Nitta (www.jetsets.jp)

take the whole world. "We are the world, we are the children. [*laughs*] We are the ones to make a brighter place, so let's start giving." Absolutely.

And yoga isn't just on the mat and even off the mat; of doing asana, or community work. Let's define yoga in terms of consciousness, in terms of enlightenment, as a lifestyle. So I'm talking about yoga in a broader sense, as a way of living, a way of being.

K: Can you elaborate on that a little bit? Because in the US, at least, a lot of people still think that yoga is done at the gym, and it's where you put your leg over your head.

D: That's amazing to hear. Because I feel like yoga is coming full circle. It came from India, solidifying in the States, in Europe and the West. Then the development of the technical details became emphasized—perhaps because of the culture of The West—and yoga evolved into the strong lineages that gave the public the impression of the "leg over the head." But it has actually evolved quite a bit philosophically and spiritually in the last decade or so in North America, and it has come back to Asia. You know there's a big boom in Asia. I've been in Asia more than other teachers who're teaching globally and I've seen it grow. Just like in the US, it was hot yoga, and spa yoga, to get people to be physical, and it's now becoming more spiritual and philosophical. Just like in the West, where the spiritual and philosophical side has grown by quantum leaps in the past ten years. But it's interesting in Asia because people are already Buddhist, primarily. People are already connected to their ancestors, people already bow, and already have a certain level of understanding on how to sit on the floor and meditate. So it's almost like they're renewed Asian cultures rediscovering themselves. That kind of brought people up to speed quicker in Asia, in terms of yoga.

❧ Let's go spiritual

K: And where do you think yoga will go?

D: I think it has to go spiritual. I don't think people should categorize the body like they categorize other things, making it separate. The physical body is the holy temple; it is the blueprint of the energetic or spiritual body, if you will. It is the house of the spirit of who we really are. It has to go spiritual, but the physical aspect is really important too. In yogic philosophy and in many, if not all ancient cultures, we recognize the five bodies that comprise the integral body, the holistic body, the experience of who we are. The physical body, the anamyakosha, the food body, is the sheath and really important. So it's about the synergistic integration of the breath and the body to become the mindful being that we truly are.

We can't just show up and be like "Om" and then stop there. It does have to be a little Jivamuktan, it does have to be a little living liberated, we have to put it out there a little bit and connect to our roots. But it's got to go spiritual and stay political, it has to stay at least environmental. Keep it to the practice and respect the lineage. Understand that even the masters before us were innovative and creative. They were daring! Krishnamacharya took major leaps. He was like: "Let's mix it up, let's get into acrobatics and therapeutics," and then his protégés took it in two opposite extremes (Ashtanga and Iyengar). Then we're full circle back to Anusara or other types of aligned, open-hearted flow systems that are intelligent, which is why they're blossoming so well. But it's that integration that's the future of our experience as yogis, as humans, as animals.

K: On a spiritual level, what do you think is the purpose of yoga?

Okay, this is kind of a long answer, and it's going to get really cosmic, and probably misunderstood, but that's probably why I'm known as the "wild" one. If you look at the world, practically all other species on the earth, all other animals, can get along in homeostasis, and in balance with their environment, but not humans. Why is it that we don't match this planet? Isn't that interesting? Doesn't anyone want to look at that? Why do we come and decimate an area, and try to control and reorder nature on this mass level of imbalance, for some purpose that comes from the mind?

If you believe that we're the only species in the infinite multi-galaxies, then God bless you. But if you recognize, at least, by mathematical formula, that it's improbable that we're the only ones, then it's possible that we've been integrating with higher civilizations for a long time. Our physical body, the animal side, is the part that fits on earth. But the higher intellect of the human being doesn't quite match Earth.

Isn't it obvious that the missing link has something to do with higher evolution and integration? That is a far out concept, but it actually makes sense. And what are we doing in martial arts, yoga, and dance? We emulate animals, and we embody their spirit. So we're really being human by taking on animal and elemental forms. Our higher consciousness, on a galactic or inter-galactic level, might seem far out, but the connection of us all, on a micro- or macrocosmic way, that's the real yogic teaching. So it's not really *that* far out. Ei! I don't know how that fits into your question, but it's interesting; the physical is spiritual.

❧ Keep it simple

K: If there was something that you wish someone would've told you when you'd started, what would that be?

D: Keep it simple. Keep it simple. I don't know if I've ever gotten there...and I'm not sad or glad, but I just accept life. "Just accept" is another very big mantra for me and it's really helped me. You know, I was out there teaching the celebrities and jet-setting, I was going from caves in India to the Mandarin Oriental [Hotel] in London and there were helicopters on castle-tops and I got a taste of the "high life." I really tasted the highest level of what I can imagine the rich life is, which I actually think will kill ya. In the end, I realized that.

From being exposed to that life, all the partying and all of that; seeing how they do it. The ones who stayed at the top of their game, the celebrity yogis that really put it out there like Sting, Madonna, and Bjork, they  Photo: Minoru Nitta

stayed with their practice. Yoga kept them inspired and as part of their lifestyle, allowed them to have those insane tours and all that intense passion and creativity. But what I learned from them as life mentors and from being a part of that jet-set world is that it's important to keep it simple. What is the "good life"? It's kind of the question that we all have to ask ourselves at a certain point. It's good to have the best of everything, but it's also good to keep it simple and to be aware of what the costs are of the lifestyle that we choose.

ᗈ Think twice

K: What would you say to a student who's thinking about becoming a teacher?

D: Think twice. That's only my advice. I would never tell anyone not to become a teacher. I'm coming on ten generations of teacher trainings in Japan in the last five years of Yogic Arts teachers and now there are a few hundred of them across Japan. And Japan is my power spot, it's where I've always been accepted, no matter how wild I was, or whatever people might say about me. No matter how honest I am, people can feel my heart here [in Japan], there's something special about the people here. I married here, I built family here.

I wouldn't tell anyone not to teach, but most of the people that have taken my training don't end up teaching. And that's how it is with teacher trainings. Most people go to get to know themselves and deepen their practice and understanding; to refine. They may end up teaching, although we all teach by example. But I would also tell them to recognize it for what it is. It's hard, especially in the early years, until you find your niche—whatever that is for you—as a teacher on a marketing level, an image level, a lifestyle level. How the world perceives you might be different than what you hope. You have to be ready for that. You have to have enough strength and power and passion to teach all day and then practice, or practice and then teach all day, or both. Because you have to keep your practice up, keep your learning up, but you also have to prepare your class. It's like 24/7. So unless you live it, love it, breathe it, feel it, all the time…. Luckily, I've had that good grace to really want to live the life. This is real. You have no idea what you're into here, people [*we laugh*].

❧ You only need to be you

K: You teach a really unique blend from multiple lineages. You were saying that back when you first started, people weren't very accepting of what you were doing…

D: Let's see, there was the Sivananda boom, the Iyengar boom, the hatha boom, and the hot yoga boom, the Ashtanga boom. Everyone was delineating into [identifying only with] their lineage. Everybody was "my way or the highway." It became a little dogmatic and it is part of our human nature to go to our dark side. That way, our light side can start to shine through. And back then, if you wanted to bring in dance or whatever, it was *way* too edgy. So I was a pioneer of the organic flow movement. But it's funny because now that I'm less interested to run around and be popular or accepted, if you will, people are inviting me everywhere. They're like, "You were the original flow pioneer" – blah blah blah. And of course now I want to stay home with my wife and kids. But I'm grateful that I lived to see it. A lot of people that pioneer in their field get exiled or even executed. So to take something and be so resolute about it… I was very clear in my moments of epiphany. "Yes, totally, it's totally related." And I'm not even talking about just esoterically related, I mean mechanically related. The mudras and the vinyasa and the mantras and the martial arts. There's so much to integrate. When you slow martial arts down, it becomes advanced physical movement therapy. When you speed some yoga up, it becomes very martial arty and very dangerous.

Rodney Yee led my first teacher training that I didn't complete. He'll even tell you, "Yeah, he dropped out!" I was so wild back then! But in that training, one thing that stuck with me was that he said that you only had one job as a teacher and that is to inspire. I always remember that. And my lifelong Korean martial arts master also explained a similar thing to me. He spoke with a great Korean accent, and was always profound and direct. He said, "Du-kan, you don't need to impress anyone." And I said, "Oh sir, is that so?" And he said, "You don't need to impress anyone Du-kan, you only need to be impressed!" I think that what he meant was that you didn't need to inspire anyone, you just need to be inspired. Because we automatically inspire by virtue of *being* inspired. It's a reciprocal process. I think that's what it comes down to; you just have to stay inspired. And you have to keep practicing, that's how you stay inspired.

For more about Duncan,
visit www.YogicArts.com

❧ CHAPTER 9

KATHRYN BUDIG

As one of the youngest and most widely recognized faces in yoga, Kathryn Budig's appetite for yoga is infectious. Kathryn mixes challenging classes with her playful personality. This is the recipe for a truly inspiring class. As an avid food lover, she is also passionate about sharing healthy, organic and eco-friendly recipes.

A graduate with a BA in English and Drama from the University of Virginia and product of Lawrence, KS, and Princeton, NJ, Kathryn found yoga in college through her Ashtanga practice. Her acting career and yoga led her to Los Angeles in the summer of 2004 where she completed the Yoga Works training with the studio founders, Chuck Miller and her mentor, Maty Ezraty. A dedicated Ashtangi and one of the youngest teachers when put on the schedule at Yogaworks, Kathryn's classes focus on finding the playful approach to the practice. Known for her creative sequences that make arm balances and inversions available to everyone in the room, she teaches in a way that encourages taking chances, opening up and finding laughter.

Kathryn shares her zest for life, yoga & food as the Women's Health Yoga Expert along with her contributor writings for The Huffington Post, Yoga Journal, Gaiam, The Daily Love and MindBodyGreen. She has graced the covers of Yoga Journal, Yoga International, Om Yoga and Common Ground. Budig has been featured on E!Entertainment, The Food Network, Shape and The New York Times. She also serves as the brand representative for apparel company, ToeSox, and ambassador for Pangea Organics.

Kathryn is dedicated to giving back to her community. She co-founded "Poses for Paws," an organization dedicated to raising money for animal shelters through yoga.

———

Chatting with Kathryn was a breath of fresh air. As her biography indicates, although she's been teaching for only about eight years, she's quickly becoming one of the most recognized faces in the popular yoga scene. She has a lot of energy and a lot of knowledge to share. She's tenacious and not afraid to speak her truth. But the most palpable thing I

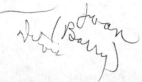

got from talking to Kathryn is how much she loves the practice. Her heart is on her sleeve and her excitement is transparent in her desire to teach and bring yoga as wide and far as possible. And in the midst of the great amount of fun that we had, her wisdom just drew me into a place of listening deeply.

❧ Not exactly a common job

Karen: How did you decide to be a yoga teacher?

Kathryn Budig: I was at the University of Virginia, I have a degree in Theatre, specifically Musical Theatre. Basically, one of my dance girlfriends went away for the summer and did a ballet camp thing that involved yoga and when she came back, she was really hooked on it. She was like: "Kathryn, you've *got* to come do this, you'll love it." So we found this studio downtown that was an Ashtanga studio, although I didn't know what that meant at the time, [*we laugh*] and we started going to class and I just absolutely adored it. It became the highlight of my week, and then I started going more, and by the time I graduated college, I was like, "I think I want to learn how to teach this. Then that way, I can have money when I'm in between auditions." And now I'm here. It was an accidental career choice.

K: So it's turned out differently than you'd expected?

KB: I don't really remember what I originally thought. It was so accidental that I didn't have any expectations. I was just like: "I guess I'm going to teach yoga now." In the back of my head, I always thought that I might fall back into the acting.

But I just started loving the teaching more and more and as a "career," it kept picking up. I can't really imagine it any other way. It still surprises me on a day-to-day basis because it's not exactly the most common job in the world.

❧ A magical time

K: What was it like when you first started teaching?

KB: It was amazing. I was really scared, just like anyone is when they start teaching because I didn't know what I was doing. I went in there with my little notebook and I'd pre-planned all my classes. I was teaching once a week at the Yogaworks Westwood studio as a–I think they call it a "Graduate Teacher" or something like that–so I didn't get paid to do it. It was a trade kind of thing, where you got a free class for teaching a class. But my theatre background came in very handy because I'm okay with being in front of people. So I got over stage freight really easily and pretty quickly. It ended up being really fun. I tend to move through the fear factor thing quickly with most things I do in my life, but I don't know, it was just very exciting.

The beginning of teaching and practicing was so thrilling. I miss it a lot sometimes. It was a much more quiet time in my life when I didn't have a million things going on at once. I had time to go practice every single day and do Ashtanga for hours if I wanted to. I wasn't exhausted all the time because I had so much energy to burn. It was a very magical time for me, in retrospect. It'd be nice if it could come back again in some shape or form. I'm not holding my breath though.

K: Were there any challenging parts?

KB: Well, financially, that was the hardest part. I was so lucky because I was so young. I was fresh out of college, first started teaching when I was 21. So I was still asking Dad for money and I could do that because I was so young. I was in Los Angeles and Dad would help out when I really needed something. It was perfect for me and I see people now who've quit their full-time job and want to become a full-time teacher. They ask me how to do that financially and I'm like: "It's going to be really hard." People don't go into yoga to make millions and millions of dollars. It's not that kind of career choice. I mean, can you? Yes. But you look at the people who are doing that and it's a very small, very select group of people. You just kind of have to be okay with a more humble lifestyle. And it can be scary for some people because there's no plan, there's no guarantee, there's no retirement plan when you're a yoga teacher. You're out there, making it happen on your own, finding your clients, finding your classes. And that's a lot to take on. I'm really grateful because I was so young at the time that I didn't realize what I was getting into, and I was doing whatever came naturally so it wasn't daunting to me. It made me immune to a lot of that stuff. That kind of helped me get over the scary beginning hump.

ᰍ **Can't live without this**

K: Do you think the yoga market is different now than when you first started teaching?

KB: Well...I think in a way, it's more difficult now because the market is highly saturated, especially in a place like Los Angeles. There are so many teacher trainings, a lot of people are being pumped out and there's just not enough jobs to go around. And it's one thing to live in a place like New York or LA where you can charge a good amount for a class or a private. But once you start getting into suburban areas, you can't be charging as much. But then again, the price of living in suburban areas is lower so it might be fine. So I'd say that it's hard but yoga's also becoming more and more popular so the demand is higher.

Basically, the people who want to make this a career, they have to want it more than anything else. It has to be that you can't live without this in your life. And the people who feel that way, I wouldn't worry about so much because they're going to make it happen. I feel that way about any career, with any person. If this is what you cannot live without, it will work. It will, it has to, it's what you love, it's what makes you wake up in the morning. But the people who are wishy-washy about it, I wouldn't push them into this career. It's a lot of work. It has become a modern day business, and you have to be savvy. You can't just be an intelligent yoga teacher and do well anymore. You can't just know how to sequence and how to teach. You have to have a Facebook account, a Twitter account, la la la, you have to have good photographs of yourself. There's a lot of marketing involved to stay afloat.

K: What's your relationship to that kind of technology? Do you see it as a necessary evil? Do you love it?

KB: You know, it can be really draining, but no, I don't see it as evil. I'm so grateful for it because I don't know how people did anything before. [*we laugh*] It's like trying to imagine what people did before cell phones. They are such phenomenal tools for putting out your energy and your work. It's great for someone like me because I can post about retreats, I can post about workshops, my articles, and my recipes. It's really nice to have all that circulating. When you're on a platform like that, it does create demand because people are hungry for the next thing they can learn. It's somewhere that they can constantly go and have information at their fingertips.

It's like being part of Yogaglo.com. I'm so grateful for that website. It's unbelievable! There are people around the world who I get "Thank You's" from who are like: "I don't have an opportunity to practice with a good teacher anywhere near me and Yogaglo is my saving grace." And they get to experience the kind of yoga that we take for granted living in San Francisco or Los Angeles. We have it at our fingertips; we're spoiled. And there are people who literally wouldn't be doing yoga if it weren't for something like that. I don't think the modern day stuff is evil at all. You're going to hear people saying that left and right and I also feel like you hear that from people who aren't comfortable with it, so it's easy to trash it. I mean, it can become an addiction like anything else and it can become aggressive, but I think that it's phenomenal. Anyone who wants to get into any career should have some savviness when it comes to online marketing because it's going to make a huge difference for your business.

❧ Change is fine

K: Where do you think yoga is in its growth?

KB: I think that the cool thing about yoga—and the drama about yoga—is that it's a very ancient practice, obviously. You look at anything that has been around forever, and the reason why it's still around is not because it's steeped in tradition. That's not what makes it survive. It's yoga's ability to change with the times. Yoga is flexible, it really is, it's actually flexible. And I feel like the reason that it does so well in modern day society is that it adapts to our needs and it adapts to our careers and our lives. You hear a lot of really conservative yogis getting pissed when they see yoga in the mainstream and it just kills me when I hear that. Because it is seeping into places where people need it more and more. And you know, outside the big urban areas, there are people still learning the difference between just an egg and a free range egg, or a piece of meat and a local, sustainably raised, grass-fed meat. All these little things that we don't even think twice about, it's all about access to information. And then you throw something like yoga on the plate. You look at yoga twenty years ago—not even, maybe ten years ago—or even today, and there are people who think, "Oh, it's that stretchy stuff." And that's the way people thought about it, it was a hippie, free-loving activity. And more and more, you're seeing it in all the mainstream fitness magazines, and you're seeing it on television and it's no longer unacceptable. It's something that everybody does. And I think all these things are great because we look to media to guide us, to tell us what we should do with our lives. And it is getting to that platform where you're seeing it more and more. I truly, 100%, believe that yoga will never stop growing. It's part of the beauty of being in yoga, and that's another reason to inspire someone to be part of yoga, because it's not a fad. I mean, will it change dramatically? Probably, as it always has. But it's not going anywhere. I think change is fine.

❧ Loopy with my words

K: In our imagination, we think back to a nostalgic India when yoga was transmitted guru to disciple; I think it might be different now. What do you think about the teacher/student relationship?

KB: I think there's people who still have their "guru" or mentor. I mean, I call Maty [Ezraty] my mentor. But I think the whole guru thing is a very Eastern approach. The whole concept of a guru doesn't really jive with the way that most Westerners are raised. I don't think it's really a part of our genetic make-up. I don't think we fully understand it. I definitely don't fully understand it. But then I don't want to knock it either because it's a cultural difference. It's incredibly important to have a teacher, a mentor, a guru, whatever you want to call it, who you believe in, who inspires you, who you can go to, especially in the beginning. It's just like having someone to hold your hand through the most bumpy part of the ride. They can get you heading in the right direction.

Yoga is such a broad platform and you can take one class and hate it, and take another teacher or style and love it. So I tell people when they're new to yoga: "Don't stop after one class, you've got to keep exploring. Try different styles, different people, you will find something that you love." The very first yoga class that I took, I actually didn't like the teacher, and I almost didn't go back. But my friend convinced me to try again and then I loved it. I mean, it's kind of like finding the right relationship, when you find a mentor. [*we're laughing*] You've got to date around a little bit, but when it clicks, it really, really clicks.

Maty is ingrained in my soul for the rest of my life, whether I like it or not! So it is an incredibly crucial part. I mean, her voice is in me. I am where I am because of her. I do have the depth of gratitude that a person would have to a guru, but I'm not going to drop to my knees when I see her or something like that. Although to this day, I still get loopy with my words when I see her. But it's 'cause I love her so much. And I am so grateful because I realize that she saw something in me that no one else ever saw. I'm sitting here because of her. So there's something to be said for the immense amount of gratitude that never goes away for that kind of relationship.

❧ The essence of what's going on

K: I love your Jasper Johal photos and yes, there's been some controversy over them, but I'm just interested in what it was like to work with such an amazing artist. What was it like?[4]

KB: I've been shooting with Jasper for years now and he's actually a really good friend of mine. Funny, he just called, asking me where I've been and did I want to get dinner. [*we laugh*] He's this happy-go-lucky Indian guy. He's one of the hardest workers I've ever met and he has the eye. He's very gifted and he sees all the nuances and all the details and really, I've never

photo by Jasper Johal

---

[4]Photos of Kathryn Budig by artist Jasper Johal were used in a ToeSox advertising campaign. Controversial for their "sexiness," the photos sparked a heated debate within the larger yoga community.

seen someone take a better yoga shot than him. He captures not only the beauty of the poses, but the essence of what's going on. Like you can feel the pose happening when you see his photographs. It's just such an honor and I absolutely adore him and he's a really good man and I hope to be shooting with him for years and years to come.

❧ No room to complain

K: You've got a lot of projects going on. How do you stay centered in the midst of everything?

KB: I'm still trying to figure that out, honestly. There's been a lot of change in my life and it's been about eight years now since I've started teaching and it's not like I've just started working hard, I've always worked hard. But all the seeds that I planted a while ago just started to sprout all at once, it feels like. So it's just trying stay with a "one step at a time" attitude. I make long lists that I need to check off. I try to check in with myself, and whenever I start to get frustrated or stressed out, I remind myself how special this job is. Especially with the traveling, you know, I have moments where I don't want to teach at all. I'm exhausted and I don't want to be in front of a big crowd of people and be the one with the answers. I want to be there and just turn off my brain. But you get there and you see the look on people's faces. They're so eager to learn and they've really been looking forward to the experience. And you have these Bambi eyes looking at you and it's like: "Okay, this is special." There's just no room to complain.

I take naps, I pamper myself as much as I can and take time. Sometimes I decide to just not check my email or I just completely back off. My father instilled in me though, that you write back to every single email, even if it's just one sentence. You just have to respond to people. So I try to. I have a bunch of emails in my mailbox that are marked "unread" that I need to go back to. But I try to fully get it done and just remind myself that there's no rush. Because it's when there's this expectation of delivery that it starts to be very stressful. I'm just learning to pace myself, learning the pace.

❧ Stop trying so hard!

K: What's the best advice you've ever gotten?

KB: Um...to stop trying so hard! [*we laugh*] Seane Corn, who's been kind of a big sister figure to me, and I were talking. This was before I'd done a Yoga Journal Conference and I really wanted to do a conference and I was like, "Should I tell them?"–I'd been working for the magazine for a while–"Like, do they know? Maybe you could say something to them?" And Seane said, "Kathryn, they know who you are, trust me, you're on their radar. You've been working hard, now just sit back. You don't need to knock on any more doors. Just let it come to you." And I was like, "Oh, okay. Really?" And she said, "Yeah, you've done the work. Just stop." It was amazing. Once I backed off, all these opportunities started coming my way.

It just reminded me that: sure you work hard, you've got to get out there, it is a bit of a hustle, but you reach a point where you have to trust the process. And you can't hold onto anything too tight because you start to suffocate it. So she kind of gave me that power, of realizing that you plant the seed, you nurture it, and then you stand back and sometimes it takes a while, but it will pop up. And just because you can't see it doesn't mean that it's not developing and growing.

K: If there was one thing that you wish someone would've told you when you'd started, what would that be?

KB: Kind of along the same lines, there's no rush. There's no rush. I think I started so young and I had a very eager mentality. There were a lot of job opportunities that came my way and when I didn't get them, I'd literally have a meltdown. I'd be like, "Oh my God, I'm never going to have this opportunity again. It passed me by. And oooohhh! What am I going to do for the rest of my life because that was the best thing that didn't happen to me?" I had that kind of mentality. I'm a strong believer of not going back and wishing someone had told me to do something in a different way. I think everything lines up a certain way because that's how you learn. And I'm grateful for all the experiences because it's helped me to understand more. I'm not really one to go back and change things. But I'm grateful for all the good and bad experiences because they make me a better teacher. Because I understand life more fully and because every time something like that happens, I have more to share.

❧ Aim True

K: Is there something that was particularly challenging that you might say was the hardest lesson that you had to learn?

KB: The whole Toe Sox drama was really hard, honestly. When I shot it, I didn't even think of it creating–maybe call me naïve—but I didn't even think about people getting upset about it. I'd worked with Jasper so many times before. I'd already shot nudes with him for his "The Body as Temple" exhibit so it wasn't like *that* was new, or at least I didn't feel like it was. So when all of a sudden, when the…well…shit storm hit, with Judith Lasater and everyone else giving their ten cents and saying: "Oh, you're a bad person, you're subjugating women," I was shocked. I'm a very big proponent of women and empowerment and so to get slammed in that way was rough.

There was a period when that was a big topic of discussion and I couldn't even sign on to Facebook without seeing something negative in my feed with my name in it. It was really draining but you know, that was also my lesson of: "Okay, I'm going to put my head above the crowd, someone is bound to throw a tomato at it." If you're going to put yourself into a public position like that, you have to be okay with criticism. So it was a big lesson in learning not to take it personally. As I go forward and start to do more things that are in the mainstream, I have to realize that I should be able to back myself up. No matter what you say, I believe in what I do.

That's my whole "Aim True" mentality that I try and teach people. The goal is to wake up everyday, set your intention, and be the good person that you are. Live up to what makes your heart beat, no matter how people and society view what you're doing. You have to stand true to that. You have to keep your aim, regardless. And it's a really hard lesson because it's really easy when someone doesn't like it or makes you uncomfortable, to change for them; so you can fit in. Then you have a lot of people not being true to themselves. I did that campaign and it was hilarious when some people said,

"She sold out, she did it for the money." Right, because Toe Sox is giving me *so* much money. [*we're laughing*] Like I'm getting paid a fortune to be in these ads. Give me a break! I mean, I can laugh at it now.

I shot them because I love Jasper, I shot them because Toe Sox is one of the best companies I've ever met. They're a tiny little company based out of San Diego and I know every single person personally. I love them and they really had a vision and believed in it. And we thought it would be inspiring, that they would help inspire people. I had to just keep remembering that point, "That's why I did it, that's why I did it, that's why I did it"–throughout the time when the muck got thrown at me. And now, it's more subdued but people still have their opinions and that's fine. That's your opinion, feel how you want to feel, but it's not the intention that was put behind it. It was a big lesson for me. Big lesson.

❧ Living with magic

K: What would you say to a student who's thinking about becoming a teacher?

KB: Find a really great teacher training program because that experience in itself is so amazing to go through. And to get out there and practice as much, and with as many different people, in as many different styles, as you can. Because it's really nice to have a big arsenal underneath your belt until you really know what you're getting into. But you know, it's all about if you wake up and you cannot live without this, then you're doing the right thing. You're 100% doing the right thing. Often when we do the right thing, it's not remotely easy. So you have to just stick through the thick and thin. But keep your eyes open and be intelligent. It's that mixture of living with magic in your life, but also having some firm feet on the ground as well.

For more about Kathryn,
visit www.KathrynBudig.com

࿐ GIVE BACK YOGA FOUNDATION

 A portion of the proceeds of this book goes to support Give Back Yoga Foundation's inspired projects.

The Give Back Yoga Foundation believes in making yoga available to those who might not otherwise have the opportunity to experience the transformational benefits of this powerful practice. They do this by supporting and funding certified yoga teachers in all traditions to offer the teachings of yoga to under-served and under-resourced socio-economic segments of the community, and inspire grassroots social change and community cooperation.

Give Back Yoga believes that the methodology of classical yoga (including asana, breathing, and meditation) is a tangible tool for transforming human consciousness. A quantum leap in consciousness is an essential necessity in today's world if the human species is to continue to exist. The experience of yoga is to go beyond separateness, alienation, and diversity and fully recognize the fundamental unity of the universe and the underlying connectedness among all beings, communities, nations and religions.

This experience takes us from "self-centered" to "community-centered" and beyond. They believe they can pass the gift of yoga, one person at a time, thus empowering individuals and building communities, and helping to reduce suffering in this world.

For more about Give Back Yoga,
visit www.GiveBackYoga.org

❧ Acknowledgements

This book is really about the teachers who are featured here, I'm merely a conduit for their wisdom. I'm so grateful to them for taking the time to talk to me amidst their crazy schedules. Their generosity and honestly was amazing; it was really an interviewer's dream. In addition, I want to thank all their teachers before them, and those who will come after. We are all connected in this calling.

My precious beloved, Daniel, not only inspired me to write this book, but also supported me the entire way, patiently dealing with excitement, fear, ecstasy, sheer panic and joy. He is a force to be reckoned with and I'm blessed to have him on my team.

I'm grateful for Judith Bhavani Cook Tucker for being my editor. Her knowledge, experience, critical eye and unbridled enthusiasm was priceless. Thank you Sara for your beautiful picture. Thank you to Mom, Dad, and Gary for supporting me always, even when they don't "get" what I'm doing. Thank you to Regan Wilson, Kim Sin, and all my friends who've expressed their excitement to see this book come to fruition. Thank you to Jeremy Douglass, Daniel Takeshi Krause, Amy O'Brien, Zoe Phillips, Coral Brent and Chelsea Morse for believing in me all of these years. I'm grateful to my students, who teach me something in every class that I lead and inspire me to keep finding my path.

Thank you to Mahashakti, The Universal, God, Goddess and all the other names that you go by. Creation is only possible with your love.

❧ Partial Bibliography

Feuerstein, Georg. *Yoga Philosophy and History: An Essential Manual for Yoga Teacher Trainings.* Eastend, Cananda: Traditional Yoga Studies, 2010.

Iyengar, B.K.S. *Light on Yoga.* 1966. New York: Schocken Books, 1979. Print

Kornfield, Jack. *After the Ecstasy, the Laundry: How the Heart Grows Wise on the Spiritual Path.* New York: Bantam Books, 2000.

Midal, Fabrice, ed. *Recalling Chögyam Trunpa.* Boston: Shambhala Publications, 2005.

Satchidananda, Sri Swami. (trans.) *The Yoga Sutras of Patanjali.* 1978. Buckingham: Integra Yoga Publication, 1990. Print

Singleton, Mark. *Yoga Body: The Origins of Modern Posture Practice.* New York: Oxford University Press, 2010.

Stoler Miller, Barbara. (trans.) *Yoga: Discipline of Freedom (The Yoga Sutra Atrributed to Patanjali).* New York: Bantam Books, 1995.

"Tirumalai Krishnamacharya" Wikipedia.org. Wikipedia, n.d. Web. 15 August 2011.

❧ About the Author

Karen Lo is an impassioned yoga teacher, dedicated student of yoga and spirituality, and the founder of Inversions Inc. She has managed a successful San Francisco yoga studio, coached other yoga teachers, and brought yoga to new communities. She has been featured in Elephant Journal, and has appeared in Yoga Journal.

Karen is a graduate of The Loft SF's Advanced Studies / Teacher Training program and a doctoral candidate at UC Santa Cruz in the History of Consciousness Program. She believes that yoga helps us come to the difficult task of being honest with ourselves. Her journey from formal dance training and performance to practicing yoga has taught her that if we start by nourishing the body, mind, and spirit, everything else will follow.

Karen believes that love can actually heal all. She is a foodie and her years of working in restaurants remind her that when people come together and are fed, regardless of whether it is yoga or a fantastic meal, magic can happen.